Lost Orchard II

Lost Orchard II

Nonfiction from the
Kirkland College Community

Edited by
ISABEL WEINGER NIELSEN

Cover Art: Linda Branch Dunn, Kirkland Class of 1977, "Still
Standing," 2019, 11"x14" collage from found and painted paper.
Cover design: Raymond Cober
Copyediting and Proofreading: Jessica Temple

Library of Congress Cataloging-in-Publication Data
Lost Orchard II: nonfiction from the Kirkland College Community
Edited by Isabel Weinger Nielsen
Includes biographical references
ISBN 978-1-950251-01-8 (paperback)
ISBN 978-1-950251-03-2 (hardcover)
Library of Congress Control Number: 2021906128
American Literature – 21st century. I. Weinger Nielsen, Isabel,
Editor of compilation
First edition
Printed in the United States of America.

Published by
National League of American Pen Women, Inc.
PEN WOMEN PRESS

Founded in 1897,
National League of American Pen Women, Inc.
is a nonprofit dedicated to promoting the arts.
1300 17th Street NW, Washington, DC 20036-1973
www.nlapw.org

All proceeds of this book will go to the Samuel and Natalie Babbitt
Kirkland College Scholarship Fund.

Dedicated to the alumnae of Kirkland College
who carry the spirit of Kirkland in their hearts.

Contents

Foreword

Fifty-some years ago, on what seems a different planet, Kirkland College came alive on a hilltop in Northern New York State. To it, over the ensuing decade, were attracted a splendid group of young women and faculty members, willing to be a part of a community in the act of becoming.

One of the hallmarks of that community was the implicit requirement to move towards self-expression, whether it be in traditional or non-traditional modes. Appropriately, the first volume of *Lost Orchard* was a collection of prose and poetry. The present Volume II, almost a decade further in to Kirkland's diaspora, is dedicated to nonfiction from that exclusive club to which no new members can be admitted. Some authors appear in both volumes.

Here are accounts of the people some of those young students have become. Their occupations and pre-occupations, professions and confessions, are all splendidly revealed. And there's input from a sprinkling of faculty and staff members as well—equally part of what made Kirkland what it was.

Savor and enjoy. It may be a while before Volume III of *Lost Orchard* appears, but I look forward to it!

Samuel Fisher Babbitt,
President, Kirkland College, 1966-1978

Preface

In 2014, SUNY Press published *Lost Orchard: Prose and Poetry from the Kirkland College Community*, a collection of poems, short stories, novel excerpts, creative nonfiction essays, and one-act plays by Kirkland College alumnae, faculty, and administration. *Lost Orchard II* continues its recognition of Kirkland authors with this collection of nonfiction, bringing together essays on subjects as wide-ranging as aging, loss, parenting, the Kirkland experience, and interviews with members of the Kirkland College

Kirkland College in Clinton, New York, was the last private women's college created in the United States, before it was taken over by its coordinate partner, Hamilton College. Kirkland had a profound effect on its alumnae, who graduated 1971 through 1978, fostering independent learning and creativity, with emerging academic disciplines such as American studies, visual arts, dance, history of science, and creative writing.

In 2015, some of the authors got together in Arlington, Massachusetts, and Brooklyn, New York, to do readings from *Lost Orchard*. At an All-Kirkland (all classes) reunion in Clinton in June of that year, alumnae authors read from their many works, including *Lost*

Orchard. I was able to read an excerpt from my short story "She Might Break" at two of these events.

In a discussion following the readings, some alumnae asked why we couldn't have an anthology of Kirkland nonfiction or artwork. Why not? The alumnae decided on a nonfiction anthology, so I volunteered to edit *Lost Orchard II: Nonfiction from the Kirkland College Community*. Jo Pitkin, editor of *Lost Orchard*, thought it was a great idea.

Messages went out through the Hamilton College *Alumni Review,* Facebook, mail, and email to gather submissions for this book. Essays came in from the U.S. and England, and a fundraising effort was launched. In some cases, authors submitted two pieces, and I had to choose which one to publish. However, I had a setback in 2017-18 when my husband, Lars Nielsen (Hamilton '77), was diagnosed with brain cancer, and all of my attention was focused on him. Sadly, he died in June 2018, and my work on *Lost Orchard II* was put on pause.

Fast forward to 2020. At Elisabeth Horwitt's urging, *Lost Orchard II* came back to life when a small group of us decided to join forces and produce this book. Associate editors Nancy Avery Dafoe, Elisabeth Horwitt, Jo Pitkin, and myself; Director of Alumni Relations at Hamilton College, Sharon Rippey; and Kirkland Alumnae intern Maria Paula Zapata held monthly Zoom meetings to discuss the direction and progress of the book. The associate editors and I read the essays and made minor changes. With Nancy Dafoe and Jo Pitkin as members of the National League of American Pen Women, we discussed the idea of Pen Women Press producing this book for us. We loved the idea of an all-women's press! Our intention was for *Lost*

Orchard II to be ready in time for the 2021 All-Kirkland Reunion, but the pandemic intervened.

It really did take a village to produce *Lost Orchard II*. We couldn't have done it without the contributors, cover artist, donors, editors, Kirkland alumnae office, Hamilton College, and Pen Women Press. I hope that this book gives an impression of the Kirkland spirit, and for those who were a part of it, my sincere thanks.

Barbara deB. Allen Purinton

Called to Service

"...those of us who did make it have an obligation to build again, and to teach others what we know, and to try with what's left of our lives to find a goodness and meaning to this life."

–Oliver Stone, *Platoon*, Quoted in *Down Range: To Iraq and Back* by Bridget C. Cantrell and Chuck Dean[1]

I first noticed them when Charlie wrote me from Iraq. "Watch for the ravens," he said. "They will be our way of staying in touch." He wrote about the moment when he realized that Raven would be a totem of protection and contact while he was serving in Ramadi with the Vermont Army National Guard:

---

[1] Cantrell, Bridget C., and Chuck Dean. *Down Range: To Iraq and Back*. Seattle, WA: WordSmith, 2005. P. 17.

1

"I was walking the final march to the morgue – and began to notice the ravens outside. After I prayed for the wounded and dead, I would see a raven outside on the way, my way, to the next place. I then noticed the flock on the roof of the medical headquarters. I also observed the flock over my compound in the morning when I awoke, and how these birds migrated to the medical company during the day, just as I did. Occasionally, I paused to visit with a raven outside the medical company, and eventually became oddly certain of their support for me. When this feeling was no longer peculiar, but a virtual certainty of great comfort to me, I wrote my wife, telling her that when a raven appeared at the house, it would be representing me. It was only two days later that she reported the arrival of a raven nesting in the tallest tree over our home."

CH (LTC) Charles Purinton, "Military Chaplains' Role in Healing: 'Being Here and There,'" *War Trauma and Its Wake: Expanding the Circles of Healing.*[2]

[2] Purinton, Charles LTC (RET). Military Chaplains' Role in Healing: "Being here and there." In Scurfield, Raymond M., and Katherine Theresa. Platoni. *War Trauma and Its Wake: Expanding the Circle of Healing.* New York, NY: Routledge, 2013. P. 312.

My husband, Charlie, was away for eighteen months on a deployment with the Vermont Army National Guard Task Force Saber. Our daughter Caitlin, at that time a twenty-year-old art college student, was deployed for thirteen months with Task Force Green Mountain. Our two older children, Malcolm and Pamela, were living in California when the Vermont Army National Guard, and their father and youngest sister, were called to active duty to support the War on Terror. I was the pastor of a United Church of Christ church, struggling to keep track of my family and figure out how to navigate the double life I found myself living. I was a civilian pastor and a military wife and mom in communities that did not understand what it was like to be one or the other.

In the briefings we attended before Charlie and Caitlin deployed, we were warned that we would all change; life would no longer be what we knew as normal. It would be, they said, "a new normal." The problem with briefings, we learned, was that it's difficult to understand all the information that comes at a deploying family, who are simply trying to figure out how to get everything done in a short time and prepare for a long and possibly forever absence.

How could they prepare us for separation and loneliness? How could they explain that we would have to find ways to live in a civilian world that did not understand the military—how could I learn how to live in both worlds?

I began to watch daily for the ravens, using this totem to focus on things of the Spirit and seeking connection to Charlie and Caitlin, who were now in places and situations I could only try to imagine. Crows and ravens are not only symbols of creation and spiritual strength; the raven is also a symbol of watchfulness. I needed symbols now. I needed something to remind me to pay attention to God. I needed to find courage to continue to serve my church and live my life as I spent daily time in prayer for my family and the Vermont soldiers who had been sent to Southwest Asia.

The ravens appeared; on the branches outside my windows, cawing overhead as I walked in the woods. On the exit ramp from the interstate, a tree on the curve held a raven. Maybe they were there anyway, but I felt them as a presence and a connection to my family. Three ravens, one lands in a tree and two fly off. I watched.

Charlie wrote that to be there in Ramadi, as the chaplain who stood by the Forward Surgical Team, praying and supporting the soldiers, was like watching your children die in front of you—these young soldiers, younger even than our children were at that time. He sent me a photograph of him in his ACUs—the gray patterned Army Combat Uniform they wore in Iraq—standing by the medical team as they worked to save a soldier. He told me how he waited at the morgue for the angel flight to arrive—the helicopter that would take the body to Germany. Eventually, the remains would go to Dover, Delaware, and ultimately to a grieving family. Charlie would stand on the flight line, completing the circle, he said, as he sent another young casualty away, forever.

I was carrying the food scraps to the compost one day when I realized what I was feeling. "I'm grieving," I said to myself, pausing mid-reach to the black compost container. Afternoon sun dappled the lawn. The woods were already shadowed. "I'm waiting for that knock on my door," I thought, the knock of soldiers often accompanied by Charlie before he was deployed himself.

These thoughts were never far away; mornings walking in the woods with the dogs, driving down to the church office, in the solitary evenings as I ate alone at the table by candlelight, nights trying to ignore my anxiety so I could sleep. When someone dies, people gather to offer support, and then they return to their routine, but not the family of the one who died. They are still trying to remember how to breathe. Church and family gathered when Caitlin and Charlie left, but then they forgot the daily reality of Iraq and the soldiers who were now on the front lines of this war. They forgot that the family still had to live with daily news reports and uncertainty. Saying "call me if you need anything," they did not know that it was too difficult for the family to even reach out and ask.

They did not know that I tried to sleep each night, extra pillows stuffed down in the bed next to me to fill the emptiness; that I went home after work and curled up on my bed, too anxious and exhausted from worry to think. I began to realize how inattentive people were to the personal aspect of these deployments. Soldiers looked like a group, and if they happened to know one, then that was the representative soldier for them, forgetting that young women deployed too, or that there were family members. I felt so isolated and ignored when "How's Charlie?" never included "How's Caitlin?" or "How are you doing, Barbara?".

Sunlight dappled the forest floor, which smelled of rotting leaves and unfurling ferns. The path led straight up to "the view" with a turn at a clearing. Charlie told me that there were some good listening trees by the clearing. I realized that the time he had spent up here before he left was the way he prepared for what would be the most challenging year of our life together, of his life, ever.

"The one off the clearing," he said, "is a good crying tree."

My life became a series of questions: What cost, then, to be part of the National Guard when the Cold War ends and a real war begins? When leaving college or job to be sent away to train for unknown destinations or amounts of time becomes the new reality. What cost to be the mother, the parent, the pastor, left to carry on, to connect the family across oceans and countries, to minister to the church? We all bore that cost.

Some Things That Remain

I cannot look at the KIA brand car without thinking that it means Killed in Action.

I wonder if I will ever not cry when I see veterans marching.

I remember the day my 21-year-old daughter put a veteran's plate on her car. I used to think that veterans were old.

I listen now to the stories that the old veterans tell, and those the young veterans tell, and those the family members tell about the soldiers who did not come home.

Ashton Applewhite

Having the Talk—Not the One about Sex, the One about Dying

July 13, 2015 - 3:52 p.m.

A close friend's grandfather is dying, though no one knows how close to death he is—perhaps months away. Even his doctor seems clueless, although perhaps he's just not saying. In any case, he's not asking. And even if everything were in the open and everyone on the same page—a pipe dream, I realize—no playbook would reveal itself. Dying is a concatenation of unpredictable events.

The one thing I do know is that no one knows what they'll want until things actually play out. This man is in his 90s, very debilitated, and immunosuppressed. He was hospitalized this week with pneumonia. As he tells everyone around him, repeatedly, he is terrified of dying. When he was admitted, he rescinded his DNR (Do Not Resuscitate order). Presumably, this means he wants any and all interventions to prolong his life. I wish his family could be absolutely sure of that, identify which interventions and when and where they might take place, discuss his hopes along with his fears. It would be a boon to his family, and, I think, to him as well. Most of the very old do acknowledge that time is short, and the awareness confers content: it's the psychological underpinning of the Happiness U-curve. My fingers are crossed.

If more people had The Talk, it would also advance my anti-ageism agenda. Denying that we will die is the culmination of denying that we are aging, and ageism takes root in that denial. The word "ageism" never appears in *Being Mortal*, Atul Gawande's excellent book about end-of-life decision-making, but internalized ageism is what this passage describes: "[Consulting a geriatrician] requires each of us to contemplate the unfixables in our life, the decline we will unavoidably face, in order to make the small changes necessary to reshape it. When the prevailing fantasy is that we can be ageless, the geriatrician's uncomfortable demand is that we accept we are not." As a direct result, too many of us die in ways we would never have wished, "the consequence of a society that faces the final phase of the human life cycle by trying not to think about it."

My friend's grandfather, alas, is the King of Denial. Only north of 90 did he acknowledge being old, reluctantly, and he seems light years away from talking about not being here at all. He's at one end of a spectrum, but he's not all that unusual. Nine out of ten people say that it's important to discuss their end-of-life priorities with their loved ones, but barely a quarter have actually done so. "It's too soon," we rationalize. "It's just not the right time." Until suddenly it's too late.

In an article called "How to Talk About Dying," journalist Ellen Goodman describes the high cost of denial. Her mother's gift on her husband's last birthday, as he was dying of cancer, was a suitcase. "I have never forgotten that image and how we lost a chance to say goodbye. I still wonder if my father was lonely in the silence that surrounded our inability to talk about what we all knew," she writes. Decades later, although Goodman and her mother "talked about everything," the topic of how her mom wanted to live toward the end never came up. The closest they came "was when she would see someone in dire straits and say, 'If I'm ever like that, pull the plug.' But most of the time there is no plug to pull," Goodman writes.

That utter lack of certainty is the hardest thing to get my head around. Even if my friend's grandfather comes around, and he and his caregivers are able to hash out an optimum scenario, it's highly unlikely that events will conform to that scenario. Atul Gawande says that achieving the death we want requires two kinds of courage: the courage to seek out the truth about our condition, and the courage to act on what we learn. "The problem is that the wise course is so frequently unclear," he writes. "For a long while, I thought that this was simply because of uncertainty. When it is hard to know what will happen, it is hard to know what to do. But the challenge, I've come to see, is more fundamental than that. One has to decide whether one's fears or one's hopes are what should matter most."

Tools and practices are emerging to help us figure out the fraught and nuanced answers, which differ for each of us and also change along with our circumstances. Gawande's book is an excellent resource. More physicians are being trained in how to talk to people about their end-of-life wishes. Medicare has agreed to cover it. Six years after vice presidential candidate Sarah Palin nearly derailed the Affordable Care Act by dubbing those doctor-patient conversations "death panels," the government revived a proposal to reimburse physicians for having The Talk with their Medicare patients.

In an effort to change the norm from denial to preparedness, Goodman and others founded the Conversation Project, a nonprofit aimed at getting people to talk about what they think they'll want at the end. At the kitchen table, not in the ICU. Not just with doctors. Also, with families and friends. Since initiating the talk is the hardest part, the organization has created a Conversation Starter Kit. It's excellent. It asks you to write down what matters to you at the end of life, and uses a sliding scale to pose questions like "I'm worried that I'll get too little care/overly aggressive care" and "I wouldn't mind spending my last days in a hospital/I want to be at home." Those were easy for me, and this one harder: "I want my loved ones to do exactly what I've said, even if it makes them a little uncomfortable/ I want my loved ones to do what brings them peace even if it goes against what I've said." Clearly, ideally, the conversation needs to be an ongoing one.

I used the Starter Kit this week because three of our four kids were in town, and it sure made things easier and clearer. It wasn't the first time I'd brought the subject up, but, like Goodman's mother, I don't think I'd actually gotten much farther than "when in doubt, pull the plug." No aggressive interventions. "What if you're in a car accident tomorrow and need a new liver?" Murphy asked. Good question. I want that liver. "It's way too soon for a DNR," chided my doctor gently when I talked to her as well. She's right. I thought I had one; I don't, just a living will and a medical power of attorney. The kids dutifully followed me upstairs to see where they're filed.

I stopped being smug about having my papers in order a while ago, as I dug deeper into the disastrous consequences of denial around both aging and dying. The amount of control we have over our final time on earth is largely up to chance. But whether we live that final period in terror is largely up to us. It is a function of whether or not we reject denial, seek out the facts, and exercise the agency that remains to us. When we do so, we help change the culture to one that is more cost-efficient, lengthens lives, allows more autonomy, is more humane, and helps those left behind to cope and mourn. I'll give Gawande the last word: "Our most cruel failure in how we treat the sick and the aged is the failure to recognize that they have priorities beyond merely being safe and living longer; that the chance to shape one's story is essential to sustaining meaning in life; that we have the opportunity to refashion our institutions, our culture, and our conversations in ways that transform the possibilities for the last chapters of everyone's lives."

Nancy Avery Dafoe

My One Hundred Sisters

Book Review Response to,
as well as Reflection Caused by,
Donald Antrim's *The Hundred Brothers*; and as symbolic
echo of the Kirkland College Experience

My devout, atheist sisters Julie and Carol; Catholic Cindy; anthropologists Angela and Leslie, who defies her professional category by always uncovering more than she sets out searching for; paralegal Marilyn; radiologist Rosa; character actress extraordinaire Katherine; marathoner Amanda, who is perpetually in training for the next big race; secretary Tracy, who used to pride herself on the number of words per minute but now on her ability to adjust to constantly changing technology; software engineers and program designers Beatrice and Betsy; politicians Claudia, Connie, and Cordelia; angst-ridden writer Billie Jean, who almost decided not to come today; community and political activists Becky and Chandra; new mothers and professional bloggers Philippa, Karen, and Sarah, who are toting infants on their hips with the balancing skills of trapeze artists; fabulist Brianna, who will not admit to what she actually does to make a living; research scientist Diana; auctioneer Amber; expert pole and belly dancer Michele; linguist professor Laura, whose husband just walked out on her for a younger, much less intelligent woman, which he will undoubtedly regret after it is too late to change the course of events; court clerk Noelle and justice of the peace Simone; dentist Zalika, who was born with perfect teeth; opera singer Marie, who it is said can break glass with a note but is never challenged; surgeons Allison (cardiac) and Brittany (vascular); Jaime, our tennis pro; ordained minister Cathy, who admits she sometimes struggles with her faith; educators Crystal, Mary Beth, Amina, Monique, and Andie, PhD; civil rights attorneys Kira and Kara; Megan, who runs her own construction business and can lift most people she meets; Brooke and Sasha, the stylists and designers of homes, boutiques, and our mother's wake this night.

Arriving well over an hour late, as usual, are Rachel and Toni, whose performance art challenges the way we perceive others and ourselves; thief and repeat offender Alisha, who joins us while on probation yet again; Rebecca/Zahara, who changed her name and race just before mother died, much to mom's chagrin (as much for the change in the name mom had chosen for her as for the unusualness of the change in race); graphic artist Gianna; Shakespeare's suicidal and immensely talented sister Judith, also ours, who is transitioning into Jude; auto mechanic Concetta, the most delicate and prettiest of us all; painter Stephanie; Anna, Alice, and Aline, whose perseverance in the face of adversity and devastating diseases demonstrates the bravery of the human spirit on a daily basis; budding rock star Kenzie;

poets Melissa, Naomi, and Gwynn, who is writing a book-length poem about our mother; economist Min; Erin and Lindsey, who are in tech support; foreign correspondent Pamela, whose last freelance assignment in Syria nearly cost her life; diplomat Emily, who just returned from Iran; dance instructors Molly, Lynn, and Aisha; editor Jo; make-up artist Eveline; Jasmine, who is forever between jobs; Jenna, who operates a daycare center for other people's children but has none of her own; historian Danielle; Leah and Makayla, whose work on deciphering codes for the CIA has made them so secretive they only speak to one another; florist Mary Margaret, who continues to bemoan the fact that she is always suggested in duplicate even when her twin is not around, but she managed to arrange all of the flowers for mom's wake, as well as the funeral, details none of the rest of us could bear to tackle; social workers Jessica, Doreen, Tovah, and Claire; on-camera journalist Olivia; Bella, retired chemical engineer, who is the oldest by four minutes and named well before the character in that *Twilight* series of books; city mayor Susannah; principal violinist for a symphony orchestra Lily; nurses Kaylee and Juanita; ethnographer Elana; cinematographer Elizabeth; grip Kimberly; television director Helen; cashier Amabel, who is deeply in love with the married manager of the store where she works; FBI agent Samantha; CIA agent Nevaeh; psychiatrist Circe, who finds her namesake in the *Game of Thrones* mortifying and secretly thrilling; animal rights activists Tanesha and Avery; veterinarian Zoe; mental health care licensed professional counselor Vanessa; and human rights activist Grace, who works at the United Nations.

All of them were finally present with the exception of Eugenia, who separated herself from her family at the age of nineteen. No one has seen her since.

14

What is more mysterious is that no one witnessed her leave all those years ago, not even her twin, Lynn. After mom filled out the missing person report, the police claimed interest but never seemed particularly involved nor appeared to be actively pursuing the case of a disappeared teen girl. Until the day before she died, mom continued to update her files and research into the vanishing of her 49th daughter, Eugenia, born seven minutes before Lynn, who is the perfect middle child with all her insecurities intact.

I like to think Eugenia joined a traveling theatrical troupe such as existed in medieval times, surrounded by fascinating people who love her. I ask Circe if I'm projecting, and she says that while I'm attempting to defend myself against the pain of the likely tragedy of our sister's troubled life and probable horrific death, I am clearly not projecting. After Circe goes to bed, Claire and I talk about Eugenia's adventures in other parts of the world. We have her in Istanbul, then sailing off the North African coast, sometimes alone and self-reliant. At other times, she is sailing with her lover, variously male then female, depending on her whim. Chrystal joins us, telling us she believes that Eugenia is actually an adopted member of an aristocratic family, like her name suggests, and she most probably rejoined her original family and is living in luxury. Chandra speculates that Eugenia ran off with some wild-eyed boy, like so many of us, and, unlike the rest, Eugenia and her man have a hundred offspring by now. None of us believes this last conjecture. At this point, I think about inviting one of my non-C-named sisters to comment but say nothing further on the subject, partially because I relish the ridiculous idea of picturing Eugenia with tens of dozens of progenies surrounding her. Brittany, however, walks in and immediately nixes the dream of Eugenia's hundred children, finding it repellant (without even hearing the whole story); Brittany is still advocating for forced birth control and arguing that all of the world's problems come down to just one: overpopulation. Despite her rational and well-reasoned arguments that dominate the next half-hour, none of us are buying her wares due to the fact that our mother is lying in a coffin in the next room.

Perhaps I should address the fact that all of us are either twins or triplets, mom becoming pregnant with her first three daughters at the age of fourteen and her last three at the age of fifty-five, her child-bearing years extending well past the age when most women are capable of conceiving. Mom always told her daughters, however, "Only have a child if you really want one." She said a woman did not need a child to be complete and that she felt entirely whole at thirteen, months before her first pregnancy. A number of us have never had a child, and some of us never wanted one. Apparently, mom wanted many, but we never wanted mom to be catalogued in some book of oddities. Yet there she is on page 192: *Woman gives birth to 100 children!* We have to laugh when we read about some woman with nineteen kids—on television, no less—as if that was some kind of accomplishment. Mom loved us all, and she generously loved many men, some were her short-term husbands, some were her lovers, and a few good-looking ones were simply passing through our port town. She always said that we should forgive our fathers for leaving because it is no small task to assume duties in a household with a hundred children. Even before there were one hundred children, they already knew children would hold the central position in her life.

Only when we get together on these rare occasions do we begin commenting on how many of our names start with the same letters, as if mom got stuck on the A's, C's, and M's, never wanting to leave those locales. I was lucky mine came near but not at the end of the alphabet where Zoe, Zahara, and Zalika reside. Zahara, of course, doesn't count as a Z name for some of us who have not yet accepted her change of identity. Now we are stuck on mom, wondering how she could leave us alone in this world. Well, discounting our siblings and the fact that we are either twins or triplets, we still feel alone. Secretly, each of us considers the fact that mom must have harbored favorites, and each of us was one of them. Yet, after mom's death, almost instantly, sibling rivalry ceases, and we become kinder to one another than we have been in years.

When my 98 sisters and I gather, it will not take place in a room filled with musty, hairy hunting trophies, nor will it be in a flooded library where pornography is the only saved material. It will not be solely in the kitchen where our imaginary brothers and absent fathers expect us to go or perhaps where our grandmothers once gathered. Thinking ahead, we have catered the wake as well as our gathering after the funeral. Rather, my sisters immediately disperse to corners, porches, upstairs bedrooms, several bathrooms on three levels, alcoves, the attic, even a bedroom closet in our planetary house because we will have already separated into intimate circles rather than factions—although each smaller gathering has turned contentious. But there will definitely be talking—a great deal of talking—verbalizing over deliberating while still listening with our third ears out of habit and practice.

As my sisters continue to arrive, they straighten entrance rugs, color-coordinate their coats in the cloakroom before complementing one another's scarves, hair, accessories.

I will stop here. I'm not being entirely forthright. Some of my sisters don't compliment anyone, and they wear no accessories or make-up. There are also stares, less sullen than those of our fictional brothers but, nevertheless, evaluative, judgmental, humbling, and disconcerting.

Tonight, there will be no Corn King bloody sacrifice, but there will be sacrifice, metaphorically, of course, because my sisters are quite capable of cruelty, just not as violently graphic or exaggeratedly physical as our brothers. Our assaults tend to be verbal or expressed through facial tics and raised brows, superiority established and conditioned with pretty upturned noses, an index finger to the chin, a teacup held as if in tableaux, a dismissive glance over the shoulder, even directly indirect as in "read my lips, bitch." That was Elana to Olivia over some long-held, smoldering grudge that may or may not have once been conceived over a boy with jet-black hair and piercing blue eyes whom Olivia discarded almost immediately after her conquest, the first of dozens of which we know.

Whereas our imaginary brothers descended to the floor, wrestling then choking one another in homoerotic, simultaneously homophobic, physicality bordering on paradoxically murderous love, my sisters will begin by automatically hugging, touching one another on the shoulders, kissing both cheeks, intimacy both genuine and pseudo. We sisters are all actors and clairvoyants by birth, mother told us, and we have proven her accurate, yet again. Without anyone suggesting, we

18

later gather in the dining room, the need for our presence before the evening meal will be intuited—we trust our instincts even when they have been proven wrong—and we begin predicting outcomes, the direction of one another's lives, without the slightest sense of discomfort until someone—Leah—says, "Enough," bringing us back from imagining annihilated futures because the moment we give voice and shape to them, the course is already altered. We shift again to comparing outfits and careers, all flattery at first, generous and appreciative, then as we change our stance ever so slightly, we notice a thread hanging from her skirt, eyeliner applied too heavily and already smudging, a run in an older sister's stockings— why on earth is Doreen still wearing stockings? A look askance at a pair of black pants that shows exasperation at straining seams; this walking indignity would be pants belonging to Pamela, who blames her sudden weight gain on an eating disorder caused by stress. Toni's emaciated appearance is part of her performing art, so her anorexia does not count.

Siblings too close in age seek out disparity then find other rooms in which to retreat, with the exception of most twins and triplets, who tend to remain together even when they are miles apart. Older sisters will befriend younger ones, eager to protect them before envying them their youth, taunt, fresh-looking skin, erect posture, and lean calf muscles, small breasts that never sag, all noticed in comparison to our own. Still, we love our sisters, even Diana and Melissa, who are drop-dead gorgeous in their forties that suggest thirties and have men and women waiting for them wherever they go. But there is none quite like our mother.

Unlike fictional, sacrificial Doug who loves his brothers and hates "their guts," neither Diana nor

Melissa will be killed in a blood-lust, ritualistic frenzy which allows new life to arise, partially because Melissa had to return early from her honeymoon and second marriage to attend mom's funeral, and we all feel just a little bit sorry for her even as the jealousy shifts shapes. Diana is about to adopt a child, never able to conceive, childbirth a biological prerogative for many of us. We have been giving birth in fields, in caves, on roads, and in buses, planes, trains, and more than sixty of us have commented just tonight on the fact that new life is joining us on the eve before our mother's funeral. This seems fitting to some of us and particularly sad to others because mom did not live to see these new additions to her family, although she has seen the entrance of grandchildren and great-grandchildren for so many years now that we have lost count.

Returning from cherubs to our imagined Doug, we sisters would not go so far as to kill one another, but we might want to pull out the hair of a particularly beautiful or extremely accomplished sister or verbally cast her into ostracized hell out of jealousy, fear of aging and death, sexual or social politics. We have also discussed our imagined brother Doug's willingness to don the Corn King mask and crown, and his uncanny resemblance to the very real writer David Foster Wallace, who did commit suicide in the midst, perhaps, of societal murder of his metaphoric "brothers." None of us suggests this kind of link to our Eugenia because, as far as any of us knows anything for certain, she is or was entirely unaccomplished, and real accomplishment is a prerequisite for this ritualized role.

This is where we diverge from our fictional brothers, yet again. We sisters, too, have stars in our presence, but in spite of the envy, something unites us in a way that nothing has before. It occurs to more than forty of us, simultaneously—and there is no need to share this out loud, rather, we intuit—we have never loved our own mother as much as at the moment of her death.

I wonder without speaking if our mother is our ritual sacrifice; mothers are always the sacrificial lamb. There are, of course, Freudian implications here, but we refuse to indulge in such psychobabble, allowing only Circe to bring up the subject; Circe, who seems qualified to discuss our Electra complexes over all those absent fathers and non-existent brothers of whom we are forever supposedly longing to gain attention. Unsurprisingly, the suppressed competition seems strongest between sisters who had the same father.

Love and hate as a dual-sided coin are as much a part of our lives as our fictitious brothers' but less physically enacted perhaps because of the children; we come back to our youth as continuously manifested in the small people surrounding us. We are capable of holding infants in one arm while balancing candelabras with the other, a chic diaper bag looped over the shoulder as casually as a purse. My sisters have entered wearing sons and daughters as backpacks or holding little hands; sisters distracted by the toddler's movements at the center of every room, and our children and grandchildren are always at the center no matter how much a particular sister tries to do a pirouette on stage. These babes of ours are so important that we lose our anger and earlier occurring covetousness wherever children walk, run, or crawl past. Even those of us who have never had nor wanted a child must pay attention to these little ones.

We have to make some compromises. After all, it is only because we take turns babysitting that any of us can even carry on a conversation that lasts longer than a sentence or two, and then it is typically interrupted by the cry of an urchin, the tear in a toddler's eyes, a seven-year-old slamming a finger between the door and doorway. Our seeming inattention to one another is really only multi-tasking attentiveness to the needs and demands of our young. Still, we manage to carry on intelligently and on an intellectual level that would surprise a number of our imagined brothers who have become politicians and policymakers who would laud our mother for having her hundred daughters and never working outside the home. They would be surprised to know, however, she did not agree with their policies and encouraged all of us to educate ourselves about the use of birth control and take care of our bodies without interference from church or state. I wonder if mother's greatest accomplishment— which was all of us—would pale in comparison to what she might have achieved had she not decided to become a mother at all. When she dabbled in painting before one of us tore up the sheets or wrote down her verse before her children dropped the notes in the toilet, we had hints that her art lied dormant. Some of my artistic sisters claim their talent was inherited from mom—not their fathers— as is often assumed outside the family. I wonder about my own successes and just how much of a role genetics played.

But, let's face it: we're not here to show off or boast about accomplishments, side with Jennifer Weiner over Jonathan Franzen (although her argument is logical and clearly apparent, and his carries such an expanse of ego in condemnation, scarcely disguised through the simple phrase, "Jennifer Weiner-ish self-promotion," in his article appearing in *The Guardian*). Various sisters are aware that Weiner labeled him with her own nasty brand: Franzenfreude, which also appears petty, and Makayla

22

states so without filter. We don't even know if we like Weiner's novels, but more than a few of us claim to like Franzen's work. Then a side conversation begins about whether or not liking the author has or should have anything to do with appreciating the work. Here things stall, then turn into something entirely unrelated as the educator troupe takes on the engineers in an unexpected battle over the STEM movement reducing the role of literature in schools, and more than a dozen of us ask why must something always be lost or terribly reduced in order for something or someone else to make progress.

Stephanie reminds us that we're not even here to complain about hierarchies of power in employment or sexism in the workplace or unequal pay for work more than equal to our imagined brothers,' although half a dozen of us wish to discuss this injustice—Marilyn, Cordelia, and Zalika continuing in this vein until 1:00 a.m. I join them around 12:45 but again lapse into remorse and silence by 12:55 a.m.

By 2:00 a.m. a few have entered the topic of racial identity again—or perhaps we never really fully engaged with this subject—or how our mother united us, and our fathers still divide us. These lines—no, fragments of discussion, continue an earlier argument about gender leading into racial identity. Jessica, who is seldom strident, is suddenly incensed with Rebecca/Zahara, but Juanita says we can never fully step inside someone else's skin. "Precisely," retorts Jess. "Her skin is white."

But Juanita shakes her head and says, "Mother would want us to get along, and what does 'white' mean anyway?". Jessica opines that she was merely giving voice to what so many of us were thinking because where does Zahara get the audacity, the right to shed her hue and adopt blackness while continuing to retain white privilege? Cindy adds that black and white are merely superficial, relative provisos about pigmentation that should be irrelevant in terms of how we see one another.

"White actually means 'all colors,'" says Angela, and "Black is the absence of color. Do you not see the absurdity of these conversations and unnatural divides in humanity?"

"Not as simple as that," Leslie retorts. "White is also given religious and secular meaning and symbolism, not the least of which implies light, purity, and virtue; black imbued by our particular society, culture, and texts with darkness and death. You can't simply assume the mantle and ignore slavery, historical segregation, lynching, beatings, subjugation based upon pigmentation."

"When the divisions themselves are false and harmful," Cindy adds.

"It is not her decision! She doesn't get to make that choice. It's unfair to our sisters." Leslie is clearly ready to knock heads literally, not just figuratively. I am suddenly wide awake and glad that Zahara went to bed early and does not have to hear any of this. It occurs to me at the moment that Zahara may simply feel more comfortable with her black sisters in our family. Then there is a knock on our closed bedroom door. For just one instant, I expect Death to walk in and introduce himself.

Instead, Alisha comes late to the conversation and asks if we are still at each other's throats. Pamela brings up an article in *The New Yorker* in which Anthony Lane wrote in his review of *Jurassic World*, "She did have a sibling, but, in a gesture of solidarity with sisters everywhere, she ate it." Pamela, it turns out, has been carrying around this issue of the magazine all night.

"Bitch," says Leslie.

24

"Thank you. I wear it proudly, but I would never eat any of you," Claudia says with a straight face, and we stifle our laughter so as not to wake the babies. I love Claudia more at this moment than I have ever loved or even thought of her. (To be honest, I don't even remember where she falls in the birth order. I am sure, however, that she is a number of years younger than me.) We are here to talk about our mother, each other, mental health issues which more than a few of us must deal with either directly or with someone we love, absent fathers, our lone missing sister, and, yes, we're here to discuss overthinking and the collective, individual, and relentless guilt of women.

Some of us are up all night talking until hoarse, when, finally, the silence inside the house spreads like a blanket of unearned compassion. As evening descends and morning ascends yet again, we remember the woman who was our mother and her kindnesses, her discipline, her toughness and resilience, her laugh, her beauty, and touch—that larger-than-life woman who was an icon yet remained an original—and we mourn. Within the hour, the first babies will wake with the birds.

In those last moments of quiet, however, before everything changes yet again, the question becomes questions and questioning takes on existential weight, and we wonder if we are any less ridiculous or grand—here, again, there is argument—yet fully as tragic as our imaginary brothers and departed fathers. There is something in the leaving that escalates proportions. Here is the ghostly twin of Eugenia again, and the sacrifices of our mother. Those of us still awake, or just waking, think about stereotypes and symbolizations—although we keep this to ourselves until Naomi tosses it out there as casually as a silk scarf—then we're forced to consider that some basis in experience is behind those waiting templates. Each of us wants to be seen as unique, special, not as a gender or racial totem.

When I finally fall into suffering from my guilt and remorse for the time I was petty and mean to our mother on the last occasion I saw her alive, my sister Christine says nothing—sometimes the most perfect, the only right response—but wraps long arms around me, and I collapse into her softness. At these moments, we are amazing beyond comprehension.

*May be read as Kirkland College as symbolic mother and her alumnae daughters.

Natalie Babbitt

Something Has to Happen

It has occurred to me recently that there is a difference between juvenile and adult fiction which is so obvious that it has escaped at least *my* attention, though I and all of us who write for children have always had to deal with it: child heroes, like their flesh-and-blood counterparts, being powerless, innocent, and daily unformed, are acted upon rather than acting. This seems simple, and yet it profoundly affects the construction of a story and defines a fundamental variance between the two literatures.

Since the child hero is acted upon, there has to be a plot to a children's story. Without exterior action there can be no story at all. Interior action—that is, the workings of a character's thought, personality, and the accumulated experience of his own life and that of the people around him—is rare in children's books. Children, and by association child heroes, haven't been around long enough; they are not experienced enough to be much guided by reflection and have very little control over their own lives. Things must, therefore, happen *to* them, things from which we hope they will learn, and "things happening" is simply another term for the unfolding of a plot.

Things used to have to happen in adult fiction, too, but not anymore. Short stories in *The New Yorker,* for instance, are mostly devoid of events. They have no discernible plots. The idea of things happening is so unusual nowadays in adult fiction that Joseph Heller could call his long-awaited second novel *Something Happened* and keep us turning the pages to find what in the world it would turn out to be. I suppose you could say that modern adult fiction accurately reflects modern adult life, at least here in safe and insulated America. Nothing much does happen to most of us, after all— nothing you could call an adventure—unless we make it happen, which fact is apt to come as a distinct surprise.

Perhaps this is why adventure novels, and adventure movies like *Raiders of the Lost Ark,* seem to critics to be fare only for the unsophisticated—escape fare which bears no relationship to reality. But whether this is true or not, there is a difference even between adult adventure novels and movies, and those intended for children. Even though the action in both is all exterior, the heroes are different: the older ones act, the younger are acted upon.

You could probably make the claim, without too much fear of contradiction, that all stories for children are adventure stories, if by that you mean stories in which action is exterior. This may be too broad an interpretation of the term "adventure," and yet it would be difficult to find a children's novel in which the child hero does not have an adventure of some sort, an adventure on which the plot hangs and from which the child hero will learn the necessary lesson. For there must be a lesson, though that is a more disagreeable way of putting it than to say

28

the hero must change somehow and thereby grow. Child heroes will always change somehow, even though they are almost always the tools of the action rather than its initiator.

The child hero who does initiate action must do it in secrecy, and always in fear of being discovered by an adult. They can do nothing overt. They know, like Mary and Colin in *The Secret Garden,* that they will not be allowed to act if their project is known.

It would seem that we are not saying anything very healthy about honesty and authority in stories like these, but they do reflect the fact that if, in real life, children are to act as in their fiction, they will be deceitful. Deceitful or forthright, however, the nature of the action remains the same: it is all exterior.

What does that really mean? To grasp the difference, you have to think about the difference between the two heroes. A child hero is, almost without exception and in spite of small aberrations, going to be likable, rational, bright, and attractive. Remember, we are talking here about children's novels, not teenage novels. Action in teenage novels more often than not revolves around a young hero's learning how to be likable, rational, bright, and attractive. Teenage novels, whatever else they may entail, are concerned at the bottom with rejection and acceptance, and their action falls somewhere between the interior and the exterior. But never mind that; the child hero and the adult hero are what concern us here.

Since the child heroes are, as I have suggested, normally likable, rational, bright, and attractive, their character is not in itself going to bring about conflict. The conflict must come from the outside—must be visited on them by forces that are big, in size and scope, and powerful. Evil and good are clearly differentiated, and these heroes will respond in ways that are dictated by their innocence, their sense of justice, their love. They have a largeness and simplicity of soul, a nobility, if you will, that ensures their successful coping. The end of their adventures will be happy. They will have learned something, they will have grown and changed, and they will be the better for it.

Modern adult heroes are something quite different. When their stories begin, they will already have been scarred by at least two decades of living. The twig has been bent one way or another before Chapter One, unless there is some reason for narrating the process of bending, and the resultant tree is a little crooked. As their stories unfold, they are, typically, themselves the engineers of the action, at the mercy of their own preconceptions and their uncertain sense of self. They will face choices, try to make decisions, and compromise again and again because right and wrong are blurred for them and run together. The conflicts are inside their own heads, and whatever resolutions there may be are determined by the shape of their own personalities. Typically, these days, they are unheroic. Typically, these days, they neither win nor lose but end, as they begin, in a sort of limbo. There are, of course, exterior events; often the heroes have brought these about, themselves, through some act of recklessness or vanity. But the events are not there to move the plot along; they are there to demonstrate the heroes' pain and fallibility. Their thoughts are often the only action there is— interior, personal, narrow in scope and, we must admit, true to life. The goal for these heroes is simply to learn to coexist with their personal demons.

Do children not have interior conflicts and personal demons? Of course, they do. And heaven knows they often act out of recklessness and vanity. But from an adult perspective, the scale is utterly different, the stakes are utterly different, the conflicts and demons are demonstrably controllable. All that is required for inner peace, as it would seem, is obedience, with all the rewards that obedience can bring. It's hard to build a story around that if you want to make something heftier than *Peter Rabbit.* Few of us can make anything memorable out of the small commonplaces in the life of an average child, Beverly Cleary being a notable and laudable exception.

And so, for our fiction, we must construct a life that is not average, not "true to life." We must construct a plot, and figure out again and again something that can happen, something that will carry conflicts and demons to our child heroes, since they have none ready-made inside their heads. Their battles will be overt, outside their heads, and, of course, they will win. Their stories, fantasy or "real," are every adventure story—always old, always new, always predictable and satisfying.

It's hard to say how long any one of us can continue to find fresh ways to tell what is essentially the same tale. This is probably the most difficult problem for writers of adventure stories, no matter who the audience and regardless of the medium. Increasingly we rely on special effects applied to reworking old settings, dressing the demons in costumes that grow more and more outlandish—or more and more subtle. But fresh ways are out there, or in there, somewhere, and the tantalizing challenge of finding them keeps up going—that, and the fact that the need to keep telling the story is very great even if, as the critics suggest, it does not reflect reality,

31

not with our stories. Problems ought to have solutions, heroism ought to be possible. In the worlds we work so hard to create, they do and it is, and if we must cope along with the strictures of the form, so be it.

Samuel F. Babbitt

Limited Engagement (Afterword)

Hamilton is, today, a larger college, a coeducational college, and, by all reports, a successful one. Historically, it is easy to look back and think that the transition was inevitable—perhaps difficult, but necessary—and, in the fullness of time, in the best interests of education. But this is a cautionary tale, and like all such tales, it requires a moral as well as a little immersion in the darker side of the matter. It can still be debated whether education has been best served by the loss of the coordinate pattern at Clinton. What cannot be debated is the surprisingly soulless way in which the matter was carried out, and the tremendous psychological, spiritual, and moral cost of that transition, a cost that is still being paid in the anger and sense of loss that lives on in many Kirkland graduates and those formerly identified with the college.

Looking at the debacle which attended the demise of several other colleges (Pine Manor, Bennett, Franconia come to mind), some people have commented that the resolution of the Kirkland story actually occurred with relative civility and without the kind of hardship visited on faculty and staff which was characteristic of those examples, such as the shocking news of immediate closure that came to Franconia's community between semesters of the 1977-1978 year. Compared to these, it is true that Kirkland people were fortunate. But to equate the Kirkland/Hamilton situation with these would be to miss a central point. Kirkland was not in isolation; it was a partner in a joint undertaking. Indeed, had the Kirkland trustees followed their urge to bring suit, it would have been on those grounds—that an acknowledged partnership, a joint venture, had been dissolved with only the coerced consent of one of the parties.

But it is not the legal point that makes the tale worth telling, either. It is the fact that in the pursuit of their own sense of security and the "right" way, the administration and Board of Hamilton not only perpetrated an incredibly wasteful act, but they willfully destroyed a lively, respected, some would even say an important college, which served the valid needs of students seeking flexible education opportunities, and that provided for the support of bright and independent young women. In the final analysis, Hamilton was alarmed by the pace of change and threatened by the philosophy that was being put into educational practice at Kirkland. Hamilton's greatest crime was perhaps a failure of imagination—the failure to see the richness it might have in a diversity of practice and approach. Many of its students saw this readily, but the institution itself was not up to it. In both these respects, the closing of Kirkland was a stupid thing to do, and it brought no credit to an otherwise quite decent, if sometimes provincial, institution.

The question remains: what might have been done? First, of course, Hamilton might have granted

Kirkland's request for limited and temporary financial support, allowing the Campaign for the Second Decade to go forward, and the college to be strengthened by new endowment. It might even have demanded some proportional oversight of Kirkland's financial affairs as the price of support. If they found that solution too fiscally dangerous, they might, at the very least, have accepted the offer of counsel proffered by the New York State Education Department or sought outside counsel of their own.

No small academic community contains the breadth of experience or perspective that will allow it to ignore objective commentary from other professionals. Hamilton would have learned, in the process, that the State Education Department had done some reasonably sophisticated studies on the viability of New York State private colleges, and that the Department has a far more optimistic view of Kirkland's ability to survive and to continue to attract students of quality. But Hamilton expressly refused to consult with anyone beyond its campus.

If, in the final analysis, and with the help of consultation, the Hamilton Board has concluded that it could only proceed with a single institution, there remained, always, the option of genuine consolidation as defined in the state laws. They could have done what they often professed to desire—they could have preserved the *best* of the two institutions in a new one that was a genuine combination. To do so would have been consistent with the vision that once led their predecessors to think in broad and daring terms about a cluster of colleges of which Kirkland was to be the first. To do so would have been to choose an option that would have maintained the support and loyalty of Kirkland graduates and their families, and the whole constituency of support that Kirkland had built into the decade of its existence. To do so would have established a specific and attractive institution, clearly distinguished from its peers. In the words of the original planners, it might have served "to propel Hamilton into the liveliest reaches of American higher education."

But this was a textbook example of the "tragic event" that Toynbee cited as the result of the failure of institutions or nations to meet the challenge. Tragic, indeed. Of course, Hamilton suffered no visible "breakdown." It went forward as a co-educational institution, and although it had the troubles one might assume in the assimilation of women into its male-dominated preserve, it is, today, a fine, medium-sized coeducational liberal arts college. One of many.

Tragedy, as is so often the case, lies in the road not taken.

Rachel Dickinson

The Wind

The wind is blowing so hard this afternoon that curled brown leaves stuck deep within the winter grass are pulled from their resting places and held aloft for just a moment before being pulled away into the hedgerow. I know that tonight the whoosh of the wind will cover the howls of the coyote that live in the gully just beyond the trees. Their howls, like the leaves, will lift up, then catch a ride on the wind and move far away from my waiting ears.

Medium-sized trees with straight, iron-gray trunks stand in the hedgerow. Their up-curved branches feather into light gray wisps tinged with hues of scarlet. They sway back and forth and back and forth as the wind pushes then lets up, pushes then lets up. The blowing of the wind seems pulsingly rhythmic, but that can't be right. Wind does not obey the kind of rhythmic regularity found in a Boy George dance party.

I like the wind and its uncontrollable nature. It is, of course, most noticeable when you're in a boat on water. Many people hate it. I suppose the wind-haters are mostly those who need to be in control of everything around them. The wind knows no master and will not pay heed to cries for help or bargains offered.

A year after my son Jack died, on what would have been his 19th birthday, I was struck with vestibular neuritis. You don't have to know what that is, only that it involves the most extreme fall-on-the-floor-and-can't-move kind of vertigo that lasts for weeks. Months of physical therapy followed, enabling me to walk fairly straight with some certainty by using a walking stick. I refused to call it a cane. I saw hills and valleys in the pavement of the sidewalk and in patterned carpet. I had to train myself to override the impulses in my brain that said they were real and trust that my foot would recognize the trueness of the surface when it landed. I also drifted to the left if I didn't concentrate on my walking or if I somehow got moving too fast. Sometimes I wished I had a video of the way I walked as a way to confirm my cockeyed movement. Every time I left the house, I had to decide whether or not I would need the walking stick based on how far I might decide to go. Walking to the post office, about a hundred yards from my house, became a monumental task partly because I had to cross a street. *What if I fell in the road or misjudged where the curb was?* I began to be frightened of crossing roads and for a while I didn't want to leave the house because navigating through the world was just too hard.

I felt sorry for myself. *Why me, why me, why me?* The line of questioning began with why did my son die and ended with why did I come down with this stupid condition? I could feel a kind of bitterness welling up within me. I was trapped in a loop of senseless questioning that had the effect of trapping me in the green chair within the Pink House. I was out of my mind when Jack died, but this, I knew, was what despair felt like. I binge-watched television shows while knitting scarves that were so pathetic-looking because of odd color choices and uneven stitches that they became the perfect manifestations of how I felt.

But the wind, the wind; back to the wind. What does this have to do with the wind that blows leaves and twigs and hard pellets of rain across the lawn in front of me? I can no more control the wind than I could control my movements a couple of years ago. But like the sailor who had to learn to read the wind accurately to expertly catch it in the unfurled sails, I had to understand and work with my new perception of space. My desire, as always, was to leave the realm of the Pink House and to travel. To accomplish that meant, once again, becoming adept at moving through the world.

Margaret Doris

Mitt's Magic Underwear and the Granny Ass Dance

TAMPA, Fla. -- Mormons are Christians, aren't they?

After all, they have the Mormon Tabernacle Choir. Not only does the Choir do a mean Hallelujah, but Ronald Reagan said they were America's Choir. They have good-looking children with excellent teeth. They are pretty much over that extra-wives thing.

Still, there is one small nagging question in the back of more than one delegate's mind at the convention here—a question most are too polite to ask, a question that follows them right into the voting booth: what is it with that Mormon underwear?

It's a question Ruben Israel and his band of brothers at Bible Believers—"Preaching at big events for over two decades"—are only too happy to answer. Brother Ruben et al. have brought a genuine article of Mormon underwear all the way from Los Angeles so that delegates may personally examine the offending garment just outside the halls of the RNC.

"You'll put on silky underwear when you put this man in office," Brother Ruben calls out like a sideshow barker. "Why don't you feel this stuff? This is real Mormon hooley underwear!"

It's not like Romney is "some wacko-Methodist," he explains, offering the underwear for inspection. It's a thin, off-white garment of some sort of synthetic fabric, with a few small embroidered designs and several large holes. "It's actually a female," Ruben says with only the slightest trace of apology, as if he's just up-ended the wrong hamster. Indeed, there is a bit of lace trim set into an edge of the garment.

To members of the Church of Jesus Christ of Latter-Day Saints, temple garments are sacred, worn under clothing to serve as constant reminders of the covenants made in temple ceremonies and of their personal relationship to God. They are not shown to outsiders, although occasionally individuals who have left the church show them in an act of defiance or disparagement. Brother Ruben says he gets his temple garments—and he has more than one—from Mormon apostates. The holes in this one were made, he says, when Mormons tried to rip the garment from his hands.

There are, no doubt, those in the crowd who would like to get a better look at that Mormon underwear. But how would they explain it if spotted by someone they know? What if, God forbid and perish the thought, they were captured by a television camera or a photographer from the hometown paper? And so, the delegates and visitors stand, affecting an attitude of both disinterest and Good Public Citizenship, hoping to get a closer look.

Karen Granville has no such worries. Karen Granville is not so much interested in the Mormon underwear as she is irritated by the fact that Brother Ruben and his compatriots are taking up her good American air. Granville is a retired nursing assistant from Daytona Beach, and she's come to Tampa at the request of her forty-something son, Kirk, who is taking a college course in photography. Kirk, who was born with spina bifida and uses a wheelchair to get around, thought that in Tampa he'd get some good shots for his class.

Granville eyes the Bible Believer display, its banners railing against Sin and Homo Sex, with suspicion. "Who are you kidding?" she demands. "When you die, you are going to be looking up through the dirt on your eyes, just like I am!"

"Woman!" thunders Brother Rueben in response, "You will live the Red Flame!"

Now there are three things Brother Reuben doesn't know about Karen Granville. First, she is the daughter of the late Yvette Cormier, a longtime political operative in Maine. Known fondly as "Mrs. Democrat," Cormier once filed a grievance with the state Democratic Party after observing, during a tie-breaking vote at a local caucus, "Some people are holding up both hands."

Second, back in January, Granville was up at three in the morning, watching television, when she heard someone trying to vault her fence. The intruder was a carjacker being chased by police, and Granville used her .38 Special revolver to hold him until the cops got cuffs on him. Some details of the event remain unclear—was Granville watching *Rio Bravo* or *The Real Housewives: Watch What Happens Live* when she first heard the intruder?—but one suspects Brother Ruben is not one to get hung up on the details.

Third, Granville is skilled at what might be best described as the Granny Ass-Shaking Chicken Dance, wherein wings are wildly flapped and a senior posterior is shaken in the general direction of the face of the offending individual. Once a rhythm is established, colorful un-Granny-like expletives are thrown over the shoulder.

Brother Ruben is only momentarily fazed after an "asshole" clips his left ear: "In my day, we didn't let women carry on out like this in public. You need to clean up your mouth and go back to the trailer park!"

Kirk Granville is his Momma's son. And he don't sit still for any Your-Momma-ing, even if the accuser has cut him out of the conversation and is addressing his Momma directly.

He rises from his wheelchair and takes one deliberate step forward. He is a large man, with orthopedic shoes that look like, if a leg could lift them, they could deliver a quite satisfactory kick to a face. He takes another step. One half-expects the recognition of a bona fide miracle right here, and maybe a few cries of Hallelujah in appreciation of Ronald Reagan and America's choir. No such luck. "Your legs are weak before God!" warns another of the Brothers.
Kirk takes still another step forward, and then another, and then another. He stops, and stands there for one long moment, staring down the Brothers.

And then, suddenly, God has had enough. The skies open, and it pours. Bystanders scatter. Granville and her re-seated son retreat to the shelter of a bank awning. Brother Reuben stands there in the rain, holding the temple garment. A banner proclaiming HELL IS FULL OF BOTH PAGAN AND RELIGIOUS holds little shelter from the storm.

Carol G. Durst-Wertheim, Ph.D.

Fred Bridge Sold Me My Pots

Some of us knew him as a grumpy, but tender, old bear. Others told tales of being thrown out of his store. Probably, those were the people who asked for and then ignored Fred's advice. Bridge Kitchenware on East 52nd Street was the first stop for professionals setting up a commercial kitchen in New York City, and a favorite shop for serious home cooks. Fred's knowledge about quality kitchen equipment was legendary, and he only stocked the best. If you asked for his advice, you really ought to have taken it.

I had been into this revered shop over the years as I built my catering business. Now, well along in my pregnancy, about forty pounds above my normal weight, I went to buy pots for a completely new home kitchen. So much potential, so many gadgets, tools, and toys! What would I need for this new episode in my life: a non-commercial kitchen, in a house, with a kid?

As I gazed along the high hanging collections, reading labels, judging volume size, seeking home-cooking sizes, Fred bellowed from his perch on a stool across the shop, "Whad-da ya wanna pay fer their advertising fer?" It took a while for me to realize he was addressing me: I had mental lapses during this stage of my pregnancy.

"Oh, I don't really, Fred. I just thought they were good pots." Such naïve innocence, but Fred had taken my measure. He'd seen me in his store before. He squinted at me and decided he would try to educate me.

"Well, look at that stuff, over in the third aisle." This was his sales pitch.

I edged around the piles of boxes, between the dusty, loaded 10-foot-high Metro Racks and into the darker aisle he had indicated, which was stacked well beyond my reach. When I was finally in the right location, Fred bellowed again, "Check those pots, triple layers in the base, copper-lined between double stainless layers, feel their weight and then tell me if you wanna pay fer advertising!"

I had not asked for his advice, but it had been given. As soon as I lifted one sauté, I could feel the heft, the balance. It was obvious there was no skimping from this manufacturer to pay for ads and there was no brand label visible either, which Fred knew. I looked around, unable to reach far without losing my balance, and realized I had to ask for help. This was a sacrilege in food service, the death knell of a woman's kitchen career in the 1980s, but the little guy was giving me a twist and kick just then. He was not so comfortable with all my reaching and stretching, and the protective instincts of impending motherhood won out. I backed out of the cramped aisle, waddled toward the cash register that was squared off protectively with counters and storage shelving surrounding the space Fred dominated, high astride his stool in the center, overlooking his domain.

Resting my bulk against his bulwark, I said, "Alright, Fred. Sell me the pots."

"Whad-da ya need?" He was hedging, wary; did I actually intend to listen to him?

"Everything, an entire new kitchen, Fred. But a home kitchen, this isn't for catering." I had been cooking forty, eighty, three hundred portions at a time. "What do I need for a home kitchen?" A home kitchen was foreign turf to me at that point. I had no idea how big my family would become. I had no idea of our plans for entertaining. I knew I was expecting a boy; don't they eat a lot?

Fred looked at me silently, steadily. For a few moments I quaked; was I to be thrown out of the store for my utter ignorance?

"Well, if ya cook, ya'll want a good stock pot. And a generous sauté, a saucepan, two quarts, a double boiler is nice, but cha don't need it. Maybe get a light weight one, just on occasion if you do any fancy baking...?"

It was kind of a question, and casually I responded, "Not much." He grinned. I had given the correct answer! I guess he didn't like fancy baking, despite the collection of gim-gigs displayed like alter-pieces toward the back of the store. He went on listing what he thought I would need, and I stood before him, nodding compliance with his recommendations. When you stand before the master, listening is often the correct response.

Fred finished his list. I swallowed hard and sidled back to aisle three, wondering if my pregnancy-drained brain would retain half the items Fred had called out. I picked up the sauté I had inspected, slowly lugged it back out to the register. I went back down to aisle three again for the two-quart saucepan, gaining confidence in my recall. Fred bellowed again, but this time, not at me.

"Give 'er a hand! The stockpot, strainer, the big sautés in the back!" He barked off his list again, rapid-fire. Lurking in the darker, dustier recesses of aisle six or seven, was another man, someone who helped find, move, relocate the inventory. Turns out, this was Fred's son. He slipped quietly forward, shy and not at all eager to engage with customers, but he carried out his father's commands. He packed my new pots into huge brown paper shopping bags, carefully swaddling them in extra bags. I handed over my credit card as Fred tallied my purchases. It was a significant bill. I had been a well-behaved and receptive, if somewhat slow-moving customer. Five huge and heavy bags were lined up on either side of me. When I turned to thank him for his help, the young man had already faded into the back of the store. I sucked in my breath and made a deep plié in order to lower my arms sufficiently to reach all the bags while retaining my pregnant balance.

Fred watched. I gathered all the bags in my extended reach. I lifted them all. I didn't turn; I closed my eyes and crab-walked sideways, left-handed bags leading toward the door. I took one step, together, two steps, together. I was a chef. I could do this.

"STOP!" I knew he was bellowing at me. Surely, I was about to knock over some weighty, tilting display. "Put them down!" he commanded. Slowly, I pliéd to gently settle the bags back down. My belly didn't move: we were both listening attentively, still and waiting. From the dark end of the store emerged his son. Grinning broadly now, the young man hefted all the bags and urged me toward the door and a cab.

The pots are still perfect. Thirty years later, when I'm asked the brand, I say, "I don't know but Fred Bridge sold them to me."

And I think of you, Fred, when my son grabs my heavy bundles, grins at me, and urges me to go on, open the door.

Stephanie Feuer

A Bench of One's Own

Crazy Horse sought out sacred spots in South Dakota to have visions. Winnie the Pooh had his thinking spot. I come to a public plaza behind a restaurant in midtown Manhattan with my vexing thoughts and works in progress. But on the first truly nice day of the year, there's someone on my bench.

She's dressed in an army green parka, too warm for the day, and she's talking loudly on her phone. She takes no notice of the buds, their fresh green trimming the bushes like decorations on a party cake.

"The doctor said I'm not a good candidate, my skin's too thin. It's a month away. What am I going to do about my face? I need your guy," she says.

I'm not interested in her quest for Retin-A. She's invaded my spot. I was loyal to my bench all winter, tipping my wool hat to the Seward Johnson sculpture, "The Right Light," by the entrance; coming to my bench in the cold, just me and the pigeons, with the sad, bare

49

twigs casting long shadows across my notebook. While the cold seeped through my pants legs where my jacket ended, I'd look to the giant mural, a bucolic scene of a huge tree in full bloom by a bridge over a friendly little body of water, and be transported to someplace where life had fewer challenges and words came more freely.

I've needed this bench, where in spring the water cascades down the brick wall topped with geometric edges that are reminiscent of a castle. The gentle tinkle guided me through tricky passages of my novel, a sound I'd never be able to hear over the telephone conversation I now can't help but follow. It's a wedding she'll be going to, and her ex will be there.

I've had other spots. When I lived in Hell's Kitchen, I often walked east to 53rd Street between Fifth and Madison to the outdoor plaza edged with a graffiti-covered piece of the Berlin Wall which once stood at Waldemarstreet. I knew a guy who, when he heard The Wall was likely to come down, dropped everything to go to Berlin to take pictures. The images launched him on his dream career as a photographer. I've lost touch with him, but I still seek out that spot when I need a special dose of inspiration.

When my husband and I were trying to start a family, I dropped a piggy bank full of coins into The Pulitzer Fountain at the Grand Army Plaza at 59th Street and Fifth Avenue. I knew the sculpture had some odd karma; the day the sculptor finished the model for Pomona he was run over and killed. His assistant finished the commission. Knowing the story didn't stop me from regular post-gym treks to give an offering to Pomona, the goddess of fruit and fertility, who sits atop the fountain. I'd toss in my coin into what I called the magic fountain and wish for a child. "There's no magic there," my husband said of the fountain, when each month we were disappointed.

Eventually, the goddess prevailed and we had a son, a big, beautiful, and colicky boy. The only thing that would calm his incessant crying was running water. I discovered every outdoor fountain in Midtown Manhattan that summer. I'd pack my son into the baby carrier and he'd wail like a demon child until he caught sight of the water. We'd sit on the lip of the pool outside the Time-Life Building or under the curve of water behind the McGraw Hill building, the midday shade a welcome bonus. I'd take him up to Central Park, first stopping to offer a coin of thanks to Pomona.

With some eight million people in the City, it's no wonder that more than 2,000 benches have been "adopted" in Central Park, each for upwards of $7,500. Donors may have a plaque engraved with an inscription on their bench of choice commemorating their spot.

Songwriter Nick Ashford, who came to the City with 64 dollars and a dream, has his plaque on a bench in Bryant Park. The inscription "Nick Ashford slept here" references a time before he met Valerie Simpson at the White Rock Baptist Church in Harlem, before he penned hits like "Ain't no Mountain High Enough," when that bench was all he could claim as his own.

I have no such claim on my bench, and the stranger talks on. Her voice cracks. I hear the desperation when she says, "He's bringing her." I know that tone and know that, though she's attractive, she needs that Retin-A, needs all the comfort and power my spot can provide. This woman needs my bench.

So, I head east towards the river to Stuyvesant Cove, a manicured riverfront nook winding gently from 18th to 23rd Streets. Each year at Rosh Hashanah, the

Jewish New Year, we walk there from our Temple, bags of bread in hand. We ball up the bread, symbolic of our sins, and toss it into the water, saying a prayer and starting the year with a clean slate.

A chilly wind blows up from the river. A seagull is perched on the low fence, a couple jogs by the otherwise empty spot. I take a seat, open my notebook, adjust my sunglasses and settle into my new bench.

Doris Friedensohn

Cooking for Change

Lucinda Holland hustles. Her small, capable hands race through the drill: opening several twenty-four-ounce cans of tuna, draining the oil and spooning the fish into a huge plastic bowl. Without breaking her rhythm, she adds chopped onions and celery, mustard, relish, and a large jar of mayonnaise. "Today they gave me an easy assignment," Lucinda says. "I can probably do this half asleep."

It's mid-morning in the kitchen of the Community Foodbank of New Jersey. Lucinda and a team of classmates, all training to be cooks, are preparing a cafeteria-style lunch for 100 Foodbank workers. When classes end at 4:00 p.m., Lucinda will catch a bus to her halfway house for a shower and then hurry to her 7:00 p.m. to midnight shift at Burger King. Five hours of sleep a night will have to do. Lucinda needs the money ($7.30 an hour) to help support her three children who are cared for by relatives in Delaware.

For a quarter of a century, Lucinda used marijuana and crack cocaine. Convicted for selling drugs to support her habit, she spent three years in prison. The drugs destroyed her marriage and family. On parole now, she does what she can to repair the damage. "I'm happy in the kitchen and happy staying clean," Lucinda says. A wry smile lights up her face when she thinks of graduating. "I'll find me a decent job and get on with my life."

Lucinda's saga of devastating loss and gritty rebuilding is a familiar one at the Food Service Training Academy of the Community Foodbank of New Jersey. Since it opened in 2000, the FSTA has offered a free, fourteen-week program to hundreds of poor people from the Newark, New Jersey, area. Many, like Lucinda, are ex-offenders or recovering addicts. Others are recipients of public assistance, recession victims, or underemployed.

Education, these students have been made to understand, is the road to self-improvement. Training is a narrower path to a more clearly defined employment goal. Still, it's a path strewn with potholes and confusing signage. Students worry: Can they do the unfamiliar book work and the demanding, hands-on kitchen work? Can they cope with dozens of rules and the authority of a white Executive Chef? Will they actually like cooking? Staff members worry, too. Their own success is measured by their students' achievements: performing well in the kitchen and on tests, graduating, finding work, and remaining employed. What must they do to achieve these ends?

***

In the summer of 2003, while working on a memoir about "my life as an eater," I visited the Foodbank and was given a tour of the 285,000-square-

54

foot warehouse facility. It's said to be the size of seven football fields, my guide announced, and it's one of America's largest food banks. In the cavernous space, block-long rows of high metal shelves hold contributed food and related household items. These goods, arriving daily by truck, are distributed through 1,200 cooperating agencies—day care and rehabilitation programs, food pantries, soup kitchens, and homeless shelters—to more than 750,000 hungry New Jerseyans a year.

During that initial, eye-opening visit, I met Robert Brown, then the Executive Chef of the Food Service Training Academy. We sat in his cluttered office, peering at one another over piles of order forms, student attendance sheets, and cookbooks. He talked about the passion for teaching he inherited from his mother. I mentioned my thirty-five years as a college professor, fighting for inclusion of women and ethnic minorities in the curriculum. We both lamented the grim culture of the ghetto and the scourge of American-style unequal opportunity. The chef, a middle-class Jew from Queens, offered his view of the training program as "an intervention"—a second chance for people whose lives had been derailed by the disappearance of blue-collar work, neighborhoods run by drug dealers, bad choices, troubled families, and limited education. "I'd like to see how it works," I said.

"The door's open," he responded.

I hung around for six months in 2004, talking to the staff and observing students in the classroom and in the kitchen. I filled notebooks with tales told by scrappy fighters like Lucinda, and I tracked the sad, half-hearted efforts of other students who seemed to be drifting through the program, just passing the time. Both the disciplined students and the drifters spoke about the impact of racism on their everyday lives. They let me know what it was like to be poor, harassed by the system, and cut off from opportunities, except for those on the street. Eager for cooking jobs, many became emotional when they imagined security and benefits attached to doing work they truly enjoyed. Some of their voices have a place in my food memoir, *Eating as I Go: Scenes from America and Abroad* (University Press of Kentucky, 2006).

Once the book was published, I couldn't wait to return to the Foodbank. I wanted to look more closely at the mix of attitudes and expectations that students bring to job training and also at the program's investment in them. On the one hand, the school's rules and rituals test students on a daily basis. On the other hand, most students are simultaneously testing themselves to see how much they want the training and all it is said to represent. That drama between external and internal forces is at the center of COOKING FOR CHANGE.

***

"You a cook?" students often ask as I wander around the facility.

"I prefer watching to working," I sometimes respond.

When I say I'm a writer, many insist that "I got jus' the story for you. You gotta write my life." I relish the students' mixture of sweetness, candor, and jive. I treasure the unexpected intimacies that flow from exchanges about the day's events—about their small triumphs and huge worries and what's for lunch. Some students tell me what they think I want to hear. A few brave souls try to explain how tough it is to abandon habitual ways of thinking, including resistance to

56

authority, in the hopes of a modestly improved way of life. I offer encouragement and give hugs. I carry a notebook but rarely take it out until I know a student well. Occasionally, I'll ask to do an interview. As my contribution to the curriculum, I've delivered a series of mini-lectures (five to ten minutes) about exotic foods and unfamiliar foodways. I post pieces about individual students and school activities on the Foodbank's website. I always need extra Kleenex at graduation.

People who cook and eat together develop family-like intimacies (and rivalries). Around food, their protective walls can crumble. Even the enormous barriers of race, gender, class, and life experience seem, however tentatively or briefly, to diminish. Feelings which might otherwise be censored are out in the open. It's just one damn thing after the next, so many students say, and the pressure never lets up. They smile bravely and try to hold their anger in check. They try not to be bitter. I'm rarely surprised when they weep and want comfort.

They also want acknowledgment—for their drive and discipline and belief in the second chance. This book is mostly for them. It's my thank you to so many students who have trusted me with their misadventures and suffering, their ambitions and uncertain hopes. It's also my chance to speak out about the benefits of free job training and job placement—even as those activities leave untouched the economic and cultural arrangements that keep so many Americans out of the mainstream.

Elias Friedensohn

Anatomies: The Ultimate Secret

Anatomies contain the secrets of existence. In my early paintings, openings in the skin display inner organs, the seepage of blood through fissures, or simply emptiness. Searching for the inner life, we peel away layers to arrive finally at the bone. Bones document history. Somewhere among my drawings of nudes is an envelope containing x-ray photographs of my spine and left tibia. A close reading of those bones documents living as the process of dying. My tibia, like the ancient bone flute, sings mournfully to me about essentials. I remember in Portugal when Zemanel served us pig bones piled high on a plate: we gnawed at the delicious leavings with a primitive passion. Anatomy is identity.

So, we are down to the bone, the skeletal truth of being, as true as the engineering of a bridge. After all else has decayed, bones endure. Exposed anatomies inspire more fear and loathing than fascination or curiosity, except for the scientifically minded who may only be concealing their morbidity. Even the neatness of surgical openings—clean incisions and flaps of flesh pulled back in a precise geometry—elicits horror. We are shocked by missing limbs, lost eyes, and extra fingers on a hand.

In 1982 in a Paris bookshop, I found a set of 19th-century anatomy texts with elaborately colored lithographic plates. At home shortly afterward, I dug up, roots and all, three barberry bushes that flanked the entrance to my studio. The conjunction of these finds inspired a series of small paintings of anatomies. The exposed innards are inventions based on the severed shoots and root stumps of the bushes that served as models. They looked insect-like, somewhere between the skeletal arches of an insane Gothic structure and the tubes of a complex circulatory system.

The roots, like pronouncements—in the form of flowers, snakes, and fruits—issuing from the mouths of kings and gods in Aztec manuscripts become messages growing out of a man's mouth. They are stripped telephone cables with all the fine wires exposed: a living communication system, an alternate anatomy for speech.

In our time, "sharing" is the trigger word: it evokes intimacy, generosity, confessionals, and sweet tenderness—even toys, ice cream, drugs, needles, and racist jokes. Sharing, once a psychologically-wise prompt to prevent battles in nursery school, now conceals power games and manipulations. "I have something I want to share with you" is a command to listen that cannot be disobeyed. You must listen, attentively—no matter how boring the tale. Sharing proposes a truce, a disarmament program as a form of attack. If sharing stops, war begins. We must share and share until there is nothing left: no privacy, no space, no self, and no name.

Sharing and war both court death. In *The Anatomy of Sharing,* two skulls stripped of flesh once

59

contained secret dreams. Now they are empty. The wall is covered with torn black wallpaper, limp, tattered flags of hope.

All around us we see anatomies gone mad. They are taking over, like cancer, suicide, and AIDS. Like primitive emotions long suppressed, they are now in full revolt. There's a figure in *Mysterious Growth, Plate III*, who resembles my younger self; he lifts his arms in surrender—and perverse pride. I think of the television technique of isolating a talking head against a flat, intensely colored field; it resembles certain 16th-century Venetian double portraits. This backdrop gives the head an exalted importance. No matter how banal the utterances, the head remains iconic. In a comic strip, the handwriting on the wall is enclosed in balloons. Speech in some of my *Anatomies* resembles an inscrutable mathematical equation: it hovers in the air between the two heads, promising but never giving. The impact of the secret on the person receiving it is dramatic: it turns his flesh into gangrenous green. Behind the figures, the wall has begun to crack. Harmony is crumbling. Not understanding another's language, we maintain a mock peace.

In a painting entitled *The Anatomy of Seduction*, the woman and man have the frozen immobility of certain neoclassical sculptures. But there are hints, in the heated color of inner flesh, of enticements. Love is imprisoned within the ancient plaster barricade of skin. The skin cracks open. Great flakes have fallen away. The walls of the room echo the skin's cracking and flaking. The male and female figures are locked together in a pyramid. Her head appears to inch toward his. Nothing else moves. True communication occurs secretly, beneath the outer skin. The cracked façade of skin records the eruption of

60

an inner process. The mouth whispers dreams. The flesh struggles to answer but speaks a different language. While painting the female figure, I urged her body toward his resistant stillness. Slanting the angle of her back, I pressed her body inward, extending the movement from the hair streaming behind to the pointing nose. This dusty invitation to love recalls Eve whispering seductively to Adam.

In the telling, doesn't the truth of a secret become a lie in the ear of another? Doesn't a painting, like life, confuse half-truths and lies—thus confounding our search for meaning? Have we not wearied from the betrayals of repetition? Needing release or resolution, we harbor dreams of an Apocalypse. There is something deeply satisfying in imagining the end. To be clean at last. And free. But no. The ultimate secret is not the Apocalypse. Rather, it is our capacity to endure, which is, at once, our absurd nightmare and our most passionate hope.

Jane Gottlieb

My House: Out of Fashion and Running Out of Time

It is springtime, a Sunday afternoon, and I am seated with friends in lawn chairs in the front yard of my family home. People come and go and pay a little money for furniture, ladders, and silly things like buttons that are displayed inside and out. The consensus after nearly two days is that this is a fantastic house, this 90-year-old white brick cottage with a yard that circles out farther than any other on the block.

These customers stay and talk; suburban neighbors I will never know. Has it sold already? They ask. They say they wished they'd seen the listing. Me too.

Between chats, I lie back and view the sky through the woven branches of our petite dogwood, a habit from childhood. My parents planted the tree after the giant old apple trees dotting our property toppled one by one through the 60s and 70s, taking up the whole yard.

Now I wondered, would the dogwood even remain standing after the sale?

After a while, we simply need to laugh and invent Hallmark cards marking this strange milestone: Rest in Peace, house, worth more dead than alive.

You can't go home again. You really can't.

Remember, when one door closes, you order more!

Since my father's death 14 months earlier, the house had been unoccupied, save periodic visits from me, from upstate New York, and my sister, who lives out west. The builder—who'd bought the place after no one else would—wasn't showing his hand. But a quick Google search found the man tears down the houses he buys and constructs replacements. "Nice ones," our agent assured us.

And ours perfectly fit the profile: located on a large lot, in an expensive New York suburb—and up for sale in a notoriously poor economy. Add to that the out-of-date fixtures and wallpaper. And, our reluctance to spend thousands of dollars to turn it into the specimen shoppers apparently wanted.

Still, I reasoned, if even one house hunter ogled its cottage-style windows, sunken living room, and dormers, the place would survive.

Built in 1926, it was white brick punctuated by slightly crooked white brick lamp posts at the street. Linking posts and house was a slate path flanked by my mother's flower beds. The setback gave the house a statelier air than its compact size warranted. We guessed our house had once belonged to the estate of tabloid journalist Walter Winchell just up the road. The long-ago history of the region involved the Indians who sold Manhattan and, later, the Revolutionary War troops marching through.

Our own history involved a dozen or so kids on the dead-end block, the manhole cover that marked home plate, and the woods we ran through to elementary school.

My parents first laid eyes on the house in 1960, after my mother found a *New York Times* listing for a "Dutch Cottage with apple trees and charm" and my dad learned they were house hunting.

But this was now. The suburban school system had climbed to the top of "best" lists, the real estate market had imploded, and there were many, many homes to choose from. House hunters were, well, specific in their tastes, our agent gently told us, and they were not interested in ours.

For starters, the front door opened to a large central room, not an introductory vestibule. Then there was the eat-in kitchen. A simple rectangle between living room and dining room, it was perfect for our family of four and perfectly situated for my parents' parties. But it was small, an enclosed space, not the family room/dining room/kitchen combo, open concept now in demand. Then there was the airy master bedroom on the first floor—not, the agent said, "a master suite," and not, "upstairs with the other bedrooms," where master suites apparently belonged. I didn't bother asking about the shed and garage, a separate barn-like building we had loved for its rafters and hiding places.

What today's home shoppers were looking for, our agent said, was, "Pottery Barn." This was the first I had heard of the retailer as a school of design. Even so, wasn't ours the real thing? It had the very sash windows, ceiling beams, and plank flooring splashed through that store's catalogues but more authentic ones.

Not that our house was frozen in time. Windows had recently been re-glazed. Over nearly five decades, my parents had replaced a patio with a deck and installed central air, garage door opener, burglar alarm, and custom shelving. A bright living room filled with my mother's Deco furnishings stood in place of the original enclosed porch. The first-floor master bedroom, an add-on by a previous owner, was a sanctuary with windows on three sides.

Recently, people close to me had died, many of them, in a small space of time. The family home was a hedge against endings; a protection from obscurity. The next owners would want to know about us and glimpse a time when rooms were small and yards were big.

Not so much. It turns out that in towns like this one, houses were regularly cleared away like the breakfast dishes, so newcomers could arrange, rather than join, a neighborhood. I noticed listings for suburban "development sites," expendable domiciles on juicy real estate.

My father was appalled by this brazen activity, once even forcing me to walk up the street with him where a large home was being replaced by a giant one—which he railed against loudly as we trespassed on the offender's front lawn. A reporter for the local weekly into his 80s, he photographed the teardown, and enclosed a caption I'm guessing his editors toned down.

And now I was party to the likely demolition of his own place, where he had insisted on living out his days, and where he ultimately died.

At a high school reunion, talk of teardowns joined updates on children, careers, and deaths. A classmate had begun a sort of house death watch on Facebook. "Ok, who lived at 300 Glendale?" read one posting, above a photo of rubble captioned, "It's gone."

A friend actually hoped for such an end to her house after her parents had died. Others, though, were moved by the poor prognosis for my house, recalling the center staircase and generous yard.

Months passed with no offers. We dropped the price. We paid taxes that were not a lot less than my annual income. We hired a cleaning person, someone to tend the lawn and plow the snow. A super storm turned the basement into a bathtub that wrecked photo albums and mired my father's WWII Purple Heart in mildew. FEMA rejected our claim on the grounds that we did not "live" there.

And so, we spent several thousand dollars having the back yard dug up for new drainage. We bought a remote storm alarm.

I got phone calls at home upstate when wind and rain pummeled the home downstate. I developed asthma as the prime home-buying season wound down. Our high-maintenance relationship—the house's and mine— plodded on.

In the fall, a builder materialized, offering less than our asking price. We tried for more money and he walked, prompting us to acquiesce. I took a walk to a house he'd built in place of another. All memory of the original was wiped clean by the multi-floored upstart with three-bay garage and driveway as wide as a traffic lane.

Talk about awkwardness. How do you tell neighbors who ask that a construction site and not actual humans would probably follow? You don't. You walk a little faster as you haul junk from house to rented dumpster, signal you are running low on time, and try for answers that are not out and out lies.

This went on until the day I tearfully told the truth to the beloved woman across the street who had moved to our neighborhood even before my parents. She said she guessed that her own house would soon be history.

And so, I cleaned out every corner and obsessed over things I found. We had the tag sale and took solace in the people who loved the place, who walked out with my grandfather's watercolors, the faded Oriental rugs, and the chairs with wobbly legs they planned to repair.

The last day, I frantically grabbed scraps of wallpaper, glass shelves, and shrubs packed in soil. I left a note asking the new owners to consider that lives had been lived here and suggesting how nice it would be to add a room or two rather than eliminate the place. I laughed at myself. I turned the key.

Friends did surveillance and for months reported no change. Then, they learned the new owner's son moved in, raising hopes the house might be spared. But ultimately, word came that the yard had been cordoned off with orange fencing. Next, our high school house death-watch reporter wrote, "Anyone live at 154 Highland or 123 Ferndale?" over photos of flat nothingness. "Both houses are teardowns." I claimed the Ferndale wreckage.

I called the neighbor for details. She described how she'd pulled up a chair to her living room window that day and watched a yellow rig do its work. First, she said the roof and chimney were lifted like a jaw, then the back came down and, last, the front door tumbled as she voiced profanities to herself.

"A dinosaur ate up this cute little house," she said. "That was how it looked to me. And in one afternoon, it was gone."

After looking across the street at our white house for more than 50 years, she suddenly had a view of the faded blue one behind it that startled her when the lights went on at night. But not for long. Soon enough, rigs were back, digging a foundation for the house that would replace ours.

I had cinematic and harsh dreams for a few weeks: The house was pristine, freshly painted and, most important, upright. Or, it was tarnished, the furnishings crumbled and family members seated, waiting for something.

Maybe it was the pumpkin-colored *faux* colonial affair twice the size of our house that rose in less than two months. Our high school reporter posted it on Facebook. In place of a yard was a driveway that nearly lashed the house to the left. Gone was the dogwood to the right. The cedar tree a neighbor had just praised, the hedges out front—also gone.

The only point of reference was a birch and a slightly askew telephone pole displaying our house number.

It wasn't that the new house was awful, but it didn't register as a place I'd ever been. The piano lessons, Thanksgivings, adolescent angst, the visits home after breakups and visits back with new boyfriends, and, eventually, children, and then the protracted period dominated by my parents' illnesses. Where was the record of our lives now?

As if speaking from the dead, my dad weighed in. Among boxes of his things, I found a prototype of a product he wished to sell called "This House: A Journal." Crafted in 1987 on his IBM Selectric, it was an attractive notebook filled with lined paper which homeowners were to use to document the story of one house.

"When it is no longer yours, whoever comes next will be grateful for your jottings," he explained in his introduction titled "Come on in!"

Ever the reporter, he furnished the original floor plan of our house, the names of the builder, previous two owners and what they had paid. He filled a few dozen pages with details about our family, the color scheme they inherited—pink and yellow—and various updates. "I still recall the quiet joy of waking up those first few days in our own house," my dad wrote of events 30 years earlier on perfectly preserved acid-free pages.

It would have been something to see him take out his pen and camera as the place tumbled down, halting the conversations-through-the ages he had hoped for. But he might be heartened to know that another use for "This House: A Journal" had been born: a precious portrait of our family in its time.

And even if I could not alter the swing of this particular pendulum, I wished I could offer just one request, on my father's behalf. Could we at least retire the house number, as we do in tribute to our most prized athletes? I was sure the new owners would have no objection. And Pottery Barn, I'm told, sells nice ones.

Cassandra Harris-Lockwood

A Little Bit of Heaven

It's hard to explain the equivocal feelings a young mother can go through. Once independent and self-determined; suddenly tied down to the most demanding and precious extension of self previously unimagined. "A baby shows you a place in your heart you never knew you had," a dear and departed friend once opined.

Surely, he was right. Remarkable and lovely was my child, but to realize a lifelong dream of owning a horse and almost simultaneously getting pregnant was nothing I had anticipated and at once was inconvenient.

It had been an uneventful pregnancy, that is, until I delivered almost three months early. Totally unexpected and born on Mother's Day, he was one pound, eleven and a half ounces. A "miracle baby," they called him. Father Hyacinth, our parish priest rushed to the hospital to baptize him with water from a Dixie Cup. It was a startling, overwhelming, and joyous time to be standing there holding such a tiny and precious one. Then he was whisked away and flown to University Hospital in Syracuse. It was a forty-five-minute drive from home.

My sister was a student at Syracuse University and had gone to Paris for the summer and left her apartment vacant. I moved into it, just three blocks from the hospital. I was there every day. I watched three shifts of nurses come and go.

It was torture, absolutely the most painful time in my life. It was as though I walked through the world with no skin on my body. The doctors told me that he probably wouldn't make it, and if he did, he would surely be either blind or retarded or have Cerebral Palsy or any number of other terrible life challenges.

I wanted to die, I grieved so, but I had to be there for him. I had to express my milk and put it in the "milk bank," a collective frozen supply of milk given to babies that could take it. My baby was so small and weak, attached to tubes and ventilators, that he couldn't eat yet.

The stress was all the worse because my family was terrified to even see him. They didn't want to get attached, so they didn't visit. My husband commuted when he could, but he was still working daily and living at home and I was living fifty miles away. So, there I was, wishing I was dead but living for my baby.

One morning I was overwhelmed. I was in the shower sobbing and crying in fear and pain. My breasts were swollen and full of milk for a baby I couldn't hold and a baby who couldn't drink. All he could take was what they called hyperalimentation, some sort of super food for little tiny babies.

I asked God for a sign. I swore that if I could just have a sign, I could make it through this nightmare. I said a novena to St. Theresa, who is known to answer prayers with flowers. On the ninth day on my walk to the hospital, I noticed the sweet smell of flowers. I looked up to see

71

that the Basswood trees were in bloom. I was praying all of the time. Was that a sign? I needed a sign.

That day, when I went to the hospital, I wandered into the gift shop. There had been no shower for my little guy. He had come so soon. He didn't even have any clothes. He lay naked under heat lamps. He was intubated and on a ventilator with IVs stuck in him, oxy-monitors stuck on him with only a little white knit cap on his head.

I wanted to get him something so I went into the shop. I must have looked a wreck because the attendant came up to me and asked, "What's the matter, Honey?"

"My baby's up in the NICU. He doesn't even weigh two pounds and they're telling me he probably won't even live," I blathered.

Thumping her ample chest, and not missing a beat, she said, "You just look at me, Honey. When I was born, I barely weighed a pound. My aunties wrapped me up in cotton and soaked it with oil. They kept me on the door of the oven and took turns feeding me with an eye dropper. By the time I was a year old," she said, gesturing, "I was this tall and this round." Going by her present appearance, she had pretty much maintained a short and stocky figure.

I recognized her testimony as my sign, bought a little music box for my baby, and rushed up to be with him.

There came a shift, an improvement in my ability to cope after that encounter, but though I went into the gift shop several times afterward to look for the kind lady, I never saw her again.

My baby's world was not an ideal nursery environment. Though the nurses were wonderful, skilled, and tender with the babies, they kept rock music on day and night, and of course, the ubiquitous lights.

The nurses were mostly young, all women, and there was a lot of turnover. In such a stressful environment, nurses didn't last long in the Neo-natal Intensive Care Unit. Many of the babies didn't make it. A few long-timers lasted, but they were mostly in the other wing, not where the newer, "sicker" babies were.

When they finally let him eat, it was through a tube in his nose. They would run tiny amounts of mother's milk directly into his stomach. I felt a great deal of satisfaction when he was finally getting the milk I was expressing.

Days after he started "eating," he stopped moving his bowels. His skin was so thin, you could actually see the outline of his intestines through it. They called it loops of bowel and said that if he didn't move his bowels soon, they were going to have to operate and take out the necrotic portion.

I was beside myself. I decided to do energy work on him. I held my hands over his abdomen and began to move them in a continuous circular motion. The Japanese call it *ampuku* when they touch you. I had learned the physical technique while studying Shiatsu in the city. I performed ampuku in his energy field and it worked. He pooped three times in five minutes. The surgery was avoided.

We had a two-pound party when he finally reached that weight, and snuck him home under five pounds, as the nurses knew I could nurture and grow him more safely at home than in the germy hospital.

By fall, we were months away from bradycardia monitors and scary trips back to the hospital. We were into a rhythm that served us both well. Up at 7:00 a.m. Nurse both sides and snooze until eight. Get up, get showered, and dress. Downstairs by nine for breakfast.

Clean up after breakfast and play a little bit, nurse a little bit, and then he would go down for the morning nap. He would sleep. I would clean up the kitchen or make the bed or a phone call.

This morning nap was never a sure thing. An hour, maybe an hour and a half, but lunch was about noon. After lunch, maybe a walk outside for some fresh air or a drive into town, but we were always back by one o'clock.

The afternoon nap was different. You could set your clock by him. If he went down at one o'clock, he slept until four. I had three hours of uninterrupted free time.

I don't know how long it took me to figure it out, but when I did, it was like a little bit of Heaven. At the very least, I would muck out the horse stall, lunge the big horse—that was his name, Big—and if I dared, even ride.

This particular day, by 1:10 I was cleaning the stall. I had Big outside on the lawn staked out and grazing. We didn't have much pasture at the time, but the lawn was lush and green.

Of course, I hadn't ridden much in a while. I had kept Big boarded at a commercial barn while I was pregnant and had friends come by from time to time to ride him. Now that I could ride, there was a constant beckoning, but as I was still quite young as a horse owner, I was satisfied to just look at him: the big, black, over-the-hill Thoroughbred gelding.

More than seventeen hands, I was told he was quite the steed in his day. He had done everything: shown as a jumper, run to the hounds, done some eventing, and was a level three dressage horse. By the time I got him he was just a lesson horse with over-extended fetlock joints. He had been "rode hard and put away wet" one time too many. But he was the world to me. From the time I was a tiny girl my perpetual request for Christmas was a horse. I vowed I would have a horse one day, and Big was the beginning of living my dream.

Yes, he was the world to me, but I wasn't quite the world to him. I hadn't had him home too long, and to him, I was just the latest in a very long line of owners he had to deal with. I was undoubtedly the dumbest, at the very least the most naïve.

When I decided to take him back to the barn, I broke a golden rule of working with a horse you don't know: Always use a lead rope. I held onto his halter instead of snapping on the lead. With one toss of his great head, he snatched my hand loose from its grip.

Looking back, I was clearly harboring anthropomorphic attitudes towards the animal, or at the very least, I had projected more canine than equine qualities upon him. I don't know what made me think this animal that I barely knew would come to me when I called. But I did. He didn't.

It started like a game, but ended in me taking one step towards him and him taking one step away. Before I knew it, he was literally high tailing it across the road and into the recently mowed corn field. Every time I moved towards him, he moved further away.

Once I recognized the pattern, I stopped and ran back to the barn to get a pail of grain and a lead rope. Thank God he had on the halter. I looked at the clock and it was after three. I didn't have much time before the baby woke, but if I could get Biggie back soon, things would work out.

I tore back across the road to find Big grazing quietly near where I had left him but as soon as he heard me shake the can of grain and call out to him, he lifted his magnificent head and trotted away. He knew how to play the "game" better than I did.

He was magnificent. His sturdy dark legs stretched long and rhythmically across the field. His long black mane flowed in the wind; his tail held high. I was struck by his majestic beauty. This was my magnificent horse. The horse of my dreams, unfortunately, was running away from me.

There is something different about the way a horse moves when he is free. Their nostrils flare, catching every scent on the wind. They carry their heads at just a bit of a different angle. There's something distinctive about them when they run. And when I ran after him calling and shaking the measly can of grain, he began his elegant extended trot, showing me just how splendid his wild-eyed, bucking runaway gallop was.

I was devastated. I became terrified as time was passing. The field was nearly half a mile across and he was running right for the outer edge. The school buses were beginning to roll. If he continued to that road, the traffic would be deadly. I stopped in my tracks and noticed that as I did, so did he.

I finally realized that the more I pursued him, the further he was running away. And besides, I was getting further and further away from my baby who would be waking up shortly. I knew I was going to have to choose.

I turned back to the house and began to feel a wave of panic come over me. It was all my fault. I was so stupid. It really wasn't the horse's fault. He was just being a horse. I was the one who had screwed up. If anything happened to this horse, I would never forgive myself. I turned around again to try and collect him. I called out to him and shook the can of grain. He took off again.

It was getting towards four o'clock. The sky was beginning to darken with clouds. The traffic was picking up. My heart was pounding. I turned again towards home and I started to pray. I prayed to St. Francis. I asked him to help me get my horse back. I asked him, the patron saint of animals, to help me save my horse. I had done all I could, and I had to go back to my baby. I cried as I called on St. Francis to help me, and walked back toward the house.

Something told me to try to get Biggie one more time. I turned around and this time Big was standing quietly with a person next to him holding his halter, in the middle of this huge field. I have to emphasize that there had been no one in sight the entire time I had been out there trying to get the horse back. If I had seen anyone even remotely in the area, I would have certainly asked for their help. Like get to his other side and help me drive him back to the barn. Something.

It didn't matter at that moment how unusual the whole thing was, or how this person had suddenly appeared, or where he had come from. I was just profoundly grateful.

I ran to where they were both standing quietly. All I could say was, "Thank you so much. Thank you so much. Thank you."

The person holding Big didn't say a thing, not a thing. He just stood serenely as I clipped the lead rope onto the halter and hurried away. It didn't occur to me that it was at all unusual. The only thing that mattered was that Big was with me and I was taking him home.

Anyone who knows horse people will tell you that an opportunity for one-upmanship is rarely ignored. A mild rebuke for stupidity or advice on how to manage a situation is always forthcoming. This person said nothing, and I didn't question it. All I had was gratitude.

As I ran back to the barn with Big, it didn't occur to me that anything out of the ordinary had happened. I put him into his stall and tore back to the house, overcome with relief. I bounded up the stairs, cleaned up, and watched as my precious boy began to stir. He opened his eyes. I grabbed him up, held him, changed him, nursed him, and went on with the rest of the evening.

There was part of me that was quite embarrassed, even ashamed about going out "to play" instead of working dutifully in the house or standing watch while the baby slept. I didn't say anything to anyone for quite a long time. It wasn't until I finally heard myself recount the story to someone that I realized how remarkable it was. It finally hit me that I had experienced what is called an angelic visitation.

I realized that the person who had stood silently holding Big had a visual quality that was almost transparent. 'He' was medium to small in build, not very tall, with sandy brown, curly hair. There was no discernable expression on the face, and, again, this person didn't say a single word. There were no wings to be seen; nonetheless, the experience was very unearthly, like a little bit of Heaven.

Susan Hartman

A New Life for Refugees and the City They Adopted

Sadia Ambure is relieved that it is summer. "I hate the snow," Sadia, who is 16, said. "It hurts my skin. I'm like a snake—my face turns red, then ashy."

Harsh winters have been one of the challenges of living in this old manufacturing city in upstate New York for Sadia and her family, members of the Somali Bantu tribe. They arrived here from a Kenyan refugee camp almost a decade ago after a stint in St. Louis. "My body is trying to get used to America," she said.

Her mother, Zahara Hassan, 38, who has 11 children, is just now learning to read and write. Sadia, a high school junior, is perhaps the most assimilated: she is obsessed with the television show *Game of Thrones*.

"The writer has the wildest imagination," she said. "How could somebody be that good?"

She hopes to create her own TV show someday. "I want somebody to remember me," she said.

Sadia's family belongs to the Mudey clan and over 100 extended family members live within blocks of one another. Family ties are everything, yet Sadia and her sisters have stitched together American and Somali Bantu identities. She keeps Steve Madden boots in her school locker to wear under skirts that were ordered from Somali Bantu catalogs. She covets Subway sandwiches—and occasionally hides one in the refrigerator—but is devoted to her mother's goat stew. She wants to try her hand at modeling, but so far, her mother, who has the final word on everything—even a trip to the movies—has said no.

This might seem like an unexpected corner of America to plant roots for Somali Bantus who have fled persecution, but in fact, they are part of a remarkable story: the evolution of Utica into a city of refugees. A large concentration of immigrants who have come here seeking sanctuary, including Vietnamese, Bosnians, and Burmese, have transformed this once-fading industrial town.

Though precise numbers are hard to come by, perhaps as many as one-fourth of Utica's population of 62,000 is made up of refugee families, according to Shelly Callahan, executive director of the Mohawk Valley Resource Center for Refugees, a nonprofit group that has helped to resettle thousands of refugees for 35 years. The immigrants have been an economic engine for the city, starting small businesses, buying and renovating down-at-the-heels houses, and injecting a sense of vitality to forlorn city streets.

"We're like every other upstate city," said Anthony J. Picente Jr., the executive of Oneida County, which includes Utica. "Our infrastructure is old. Our housing stock is old. But the refugees have renovated and revitalized whole neighborhoods."

Utica became a refugee magnet mostly by accident. In the 1970s, a local woman, Roberta Douglas, became concerned about the treatment of Amerasian children in Vietnam. So, with the help of Catholic Charities in Syracuse, she started resettling Amerasians and later, working with others, established the Center for Refugees.

The center, which provide assistance with housing, employment, cultural orientation, and language skills, works with the Lutheran Immigration and Refugee Service and the federal government to determine which refugee groups will be resettled in Utica. People are granted refugee status generally because they are fleeing persecution for a variety of reasons, including race and religion.

The refugees now carving out new lives are just the latest surge of immigrants to the city. At the turn of the century, Italian, German, Polish, and Irish immigrants were drawn to Utica's mills, and many started their own businesses.

"My grandfather was the first gentleman to walk up and down the streets of Utica yelling, 'Lemon ices!'" said Anthony Amodio, 48, the food and beverage manager at the Radisson Hotel Utica Center. Later, his grandfather opened a salumeria.

Syrian and Lebanese immigrants arrived around the same time and eventually opened dry goods stores and groceries.

General Electric, Univac, a computer manufacturer, and Griffiss Air Force Base provided thousands of jobs after the mills closed in the 1950s. But in a narrative familiar across upstate New York, the manufacturing plants started downsizing before eventually closing—the Air Force base also closed—and the city fell into a steep decline. The population, which stood at 100,000 in 1960, plunged, and Genesee, the city's gracious main street, filled with empty storefronts.

Residents still recall a popular bumper sticker: "Last one out of Utica, please turn out the lights."

"The refugees stemmed the decline," Ms. Callahan said. "They have a great work ethic and are willing to take jobs that native-born folks don't want."

These days, many work as dishwashers, groundskeepers, janitors, and housekeepers at Turning Stone Resort and Casino in Verona, N.Y., while others have found work at a Chobani yogurt factory in New Berlin, N.Y, owned by a Turkish immigrant.

The Bosnians, who started arriving in the early 1990s during the Balkan conflict and are Utica's largest refugee community, have been arguably the most successful group. They have bought and renovated hundreds of run-down houses, started construction firms, opened restaurants, and built a soaring mosque.

"All of us had everything," Sefik Badnjevic, 58, a retired machinist, said, referring to the many middle-class lives uprooted by war. "We are trying to make what we lost."

Two refugee groups that have been in Utica for more than a generation have also done well: Vietnamese have opened restaurants and food stores, while Russians who escaped religious persecution in the former Soviet Union have opened furniture stores and car dealerships.

For more recent arrivals, many of whom were living in refugee camps, "the learning curve has been longer, slower," Ms. Callahan said.

Yet the Karen, a persecuted ethnic group from the Karen state in southeastern Burma who started arriving in Utica a decade ago, have established a foothold, opening markets and buying homes.

The Somali Bantus, however, have had a tougher time adapting. For many, there is a deep sense of dislocation. They were brought to Somalia as slaves from other African countries by Arab slave traders centuries ago. A civil war forced them to flee in the early 1990s to crowded Kenyan refugee camps.

In 2003, 61 Somali Bantus were resettled in Utica; the community has since grown to about 2,000.

"The teachers send home letters about the kids, but the parents can't read them," said Mohamed Ganiso, 33, the director of the Somali Bantu Association of Central New York in Utica. "If they apply for a job, they're told to go online, but they can't."

Mr. Ganiso, who works as a machine operator at Chobani, estimated that unemployment in the Somali Bantu community runs about 50 percent.

But for the Bantus, there is still a sense of accomplishment—and of possibilities.

Sadia admires her mother's strength and independence. "She raised us all by herself," the daughter said.

It has not been easy. Ms. Hassan was a nursing home aide for six years then worked at the Chobani factory for a year. Despite the 12-hour factory shifts, she relished the job, especially the camaraderie. "We had two families—our Chobani family and our home family," Ms. Hassan said.

She quit after her daughter Rahama was born last September, not wanting to be away from home for such long stretches. But Ms. Hassan misses the work and the paycheck. "We felt rich," Sadia said.

She and her mother are close and often banter. "I have a secret boyfriend," Sadia told her mother recently. "Shame on you!" Ms. Hassan shot back, knowing her daughter was joking. But she was worried: there is no dating in Somali Bantu culture unless a couple is engaged.

But a year ago, Sadia was angry with her family. "If I want to become a model, they won't let me," she said. "If I want to go to Syracuse University, they won't let me."

She stopped speaking to her mother and started having problems at school. Sadia's principal called her into his office.

"He made me understand," she said. "'Nobody's ever going to love you better than your mom.'"

Still, the moments of challenge and tension pale compared with what the family left behind.

During the 12 years her family spent in a refugee camp, "we slept on the floor," Ms. Hassan said, as she sat in the living room of her house, a former drug rehabilitation center she bought in 2010 for $55,000.

Rations were meager at the camp. "Dried corn, beans—no rice, a little oil," she said. Armed members of the Turkana, a semi-nomadic Kenyan tribe, often stole food and clothing at night. Women going into the forest alone for firewood risked being raped.

Now in their own yard, Ms. Hassan's daughter Mana Abdika Dir Mudey, 20, a student at Mohawk Valley Community College who is planning to become a nurse, hung freshly washed sheets on a line. In the kitchen, Ms. Hassan's mother, Halima Mudey, 58, cooked stew.

Looking around, Ms. Hassan said simply, "Here, we have everything."

Martha Hawley

La Celestina: Lost Conversations

I remember the buzz: farmers in the Clinton, New York, area were outraged about the land clearance for the construction of Kirkland College. At least one farmer had vented his anger, stating that his livestock had been cursed by the wild, noisy female students. One animal had just up and died in the forest. Apple orchards had started to fail as soon as the first Kirkland students arrived in town. Jokes were exchanged about ranting farmers, pitchforks in hand. Factual? In certain quarters, mistrust has beyond a doubt surfaced in different measures from time to time.

December 1972: Rita Pa abandoned her nocturnal practice of sculpting to help me retype my senior paper: "*La Celestina*: A Literary Synthesis of 15th-Century Attitudes towards Witchcraft in Spain and France." By the time the Class of '73 was graduating, I had made my first pilgrimage, in the company of Constance Stellas '72, to Cordoba in southern Spain, once home to Arab, Jewish, and Christian scholars. Life in *Al-Andalus* before the Catholic *reconquista* of Iberia

85

was not as harmonious as some have claimed, but the diverse traditions once there have shaped society in Spain for a thousand years.

La Celestina (1499), by Fernando de Rojas, is categorized as dramatic writing, a novel in dialogue form or a prose drama in dialogue. The character of Celestina has become Spain's best-known madam, bawd, procuress, go-between, and witch. Rojas' work appeared at the start of Spain's Golden Age, the *Siglo de Oro*. Five hundred years on, his hometown of La Puebla de Montalbán hosts the annual Celestina Festival, and its Celestina Museum is open year-round. Celestina has inspired artists from Goya to Picasso; the work is still required reading in Spanish schools; film and opera carry the name forward; being a *Celestina* has entered the language like the term for a *Don Juan*. Modern adaptations of the tale of lust, greed, and murder have been staged by Robert Lepage ("brimming over with classical lore and a salty wisdom gained in the course of a vigorous and sinful life," program notes 2004-5) and Calixto Bieito (who set his 2004 production in a tough neighborhood on the edges of Barcelona, a "landscape of cheap prostitution"). *Celestinistas* meet at conferences, and *La Celestina* restaurants can be found on several continents.

The Rojas' themes of wealth and poverty, inequality, and injustice have endured. The title and plot twists change from the earliest version (1499) onwards, but the basic story is this:

Calisto, a young nobleman, falls in love with the chaste Melibea. His servant Sempronio points him in the direction of Celestina, a well-known go-between, witch, and virgin-mender. Calisto contacts Celestina, who agrees to work her magic on Melibea, for a price.

Sempronio and fellow-servant Pármeno are now in cahoots, hoping to cash in on the high fee paid to Celestina. They visit her, clash over rewards, and murder Celestina, only to be put to death for their deeds. This line of work entailed dealing with members of high society, for whom escape from the boundaries of a rigid moral code could result in loss of position and punishment for excessive deviation. Celestina herself was considered a deviant and an influential one at that, much sought after throughout the city, provoking reactions that stemmed from deep within the psyche of her opponents.

Attitudes towards females in the 15th century, magic, and the devil affirm the idea that women, believed to be weaker, were simply more likely to submit to Satan's advances. In the early 16th century, Fray Martin de Castañega wrote that women, having no bona fide reason for holding knowledge of the sciences and medicine, were automatically suspect if found dabbling in the field. They were to be apprehended and executed.

Meanwhile, Calisto does manage to seduce Melibea but falls to his death while scaling a wall as he departs. Melibea, in despair, commits suicide.

Back to 1972, and about 15% of that senior paper (minus footnotes, you'll be glad to know):

> My discussion bases itself on the premise *La Celestina*, the Spanish drama which begins Spain's *siglo de oro*, offers Celestina herself as a literary synthesis of attitudes towards witchcraft in the 15th century. Due to her traditional representation as the urban eccentric, dabbling in arts concerning potions and herbs, while guided by a keen mentality which enables her to survive by utilizing

numerous professional skills, Celestina has not often been discussed from the perspective of her witch-like qualities.

Celestina is a favorite stereotype worthy of scorn: an old, unkempt woman, known by all, yet befriended by few. Her sagacity, as described by Pármeno, is due to "need and poverty, hunger." Celestina found fame through her great prowess as a sorceress, a manufacturess of charms and potions which served to cure physical ailments, from toothaches to the mending of maidenheads. She also relieved sexual frustrations by arranging reunions of potential romantic partners...

By 1398, the faculty of the University of Paris had decided that witchcraft involved a pact with the Devil. However, there was confusion between those who were at his service and those who held him at their command. Celestina belongs to neither category but assumes command over the Devil while formulating her pact and is bold enough to threaten him if he does not follow her wishes. Rather than being an indication of her actual allegiance to the Christian God, since command over the Devil implied true faith, this pact is representative of the period in Spain when the question of differentiation between sorcery and witchcraft was still undecided.

A general distinction can be made between witchcraft in Spain and France.

The mystical heritage of Spain, handed down from the Moors, Jews, and Gypsies, allowed for a delay in their persecution. Geography and political isolation allowed astrology and necromancy to be offered as formal courses at Spanish universities, not long before the first witch was burned in France. The expulsion of the Jews and debasement of the Moors coincided with massive burnings of their works related to magic and a movement towards the outlawing of occult practices. While more heretics were burned in Spain than in any other European country, the actual period of witchcraft trials was shorter in Spain than in France. Due to the total reorganization and unification of Spain— which began at the end of the 15th century—secular courts in Spain wielded considerably less power than in France, where the first witchcraft trial by a secular court was held in 1390.

From the 13th century onward, theologians were redefining the identity of Satan, and ideas related to a detailed concept of the pact with the Devil were elaborated upon by many whose writings classified them as 'demonologists.' Alphonsus de Spina, an important demonologist and inquisitor, wrote the *Fortalicum Fidei*, concerning the threat of anti-Catholic forces in Spain during the mid-15th century. Although his book is moderate in comparison with persuasive works that followed, he discusses the war against Jews, Saracens (or Mohamme-dans), and demons, and has been seen as the single most influential contributor to the cause of race-hatred in 15th century Spain.

While Celestina exhibits many instances of mockery of the Church, she is well schooled in the art of feigning reverence. She feared punishment for her work, and while secretly proud of her success, she does not reveal her diabolic past at random. During a time when loss of virginity incurred heavy and long-term castigation for a young woman, the skill of mending broken maidenheads is not to be underestimated in its importance in Celestina's roster of services rendered. The need for secretive behavior corresponds to the historical belief that the activities of witches were hidden and mysterious. This idea was behind thousands of women burned for their "crimes" because it was held that evidence could not be gathered and was therefore unnecessary. The number of confessions obtained from witches can partly be attributed to systematic torture.

Celestina, as wretched as the next when it came to identifying old, persecuted people on the street, lived with her own variety of folk religion which reduced God from his position of ruler to that of minor spirit. She addresses Satan

90

as Sir, Emperor, Captain, Governor, Commander, Administrator, Breadwinner. The pact can be seen as a continuance of pagan relationships which often entailed individualized relationships with deities.

A sizable gap existed between upper-class views of witchcraft, in theological doctrine and artistic interpretation, and a common trans-ference of beliefs from one generation to the next. Pagan rituals, deities, calendar, and meeting places were co-opted by the Christian Church in the attempt to convert all conquered peoples to Christianity, but such standardization was slow and accommodated the survival of aspects of pagan worship. Certain heresies which arose during the Middle Ages were banned as resistance from within the Church, but witchcraft, isolated because of its homage paid to the Kingdom of Evil, was an outside threat.

In 2016, I wonder, was the angry farmer scenario no more than a rumor? I feel like it really happened, but I'll settle for pegging it as useful hearsay, especially if its recall evokes levity rather than loss. Besides, we understand more now about what triggers fear. Right?

Rev. Alice Hildebrand

Lengthening Out

Once during a visit with some lobstering friends, I asked them if their son was still fishing, or if he had hauled his traps for the year. They told me that he'd be fishing through the winter, saying, "Right now he's lengthening out." I could immediately envision what was being talked about: lengthening out the pot warps with extra pieces of line so that the traps could be set in deeper water, further offshore. When winter storms come and the waters grow more turbulent close to land, the lobsters head out. As I sat in quietness one morning this week, clearing my head of the clamor of all that needs to be done in the next few months, that phrase, "lengthening out," came to me. In times of turmoil, when the waters of our own personal seas are stormy, or when the waters of the world lash against us, we need to lengthen out—lengthen our spiritual moorings. We need to set our traps in deeper water in order to catch spiritual food.

Scriptures, from Job and from Luke, are both written about stormy times. Luke wrote his Gospel about ten years after the destruction of Jerusalem and the

Temple there by the Romans. A million people had died. The razing of the Temple was the final proof to the Jews that their efforts to break free of Roman tyranny were useless. They were defeated. But in the verses, Jesus reassures his hearers that despite any tribulation, "by your endurance you will gain your souls." We could say that the entire book of Job is a reflection upon that theme—gaining one's soul by endurance. This process of endurance is akin to what I mean when I say we need to lengthen out our spiritual moorings. We can't control the conditions of our lives; we can't avoid stormy weather or times of suffering and uncertainty. But we seek to understand our lot; we need love and companionship while we search for meaning.

Recently a friend disagreed with my opinion that science and religion are alike concerned with the "why's and wherefore's" of human existence. No, he said, science doesn't ask "why?". I realized as we spoke that he was right—science asks "how?". It is to religion that we often turn with our "why?" questions. In my work as a chaplain, at a big city hospital in Hartford, Connecticut, a medical center with 955 beds that was a referral point of last resort for people from all over New England, as well as for the inner-city poor who surrounded it, and again at Maine Medical Center in Portland, the same kind of setting but on a smaller scale, and now as a volunteer chaplain at St Joe's on Bangor, I meet suffering over and over again, and the endurance that brings people through it. In a modern hospital, all around us is the highly sophisticated care mechanism of today's medicine, asking and answering one "how" question after another. How can we alleviate this symptom, how can we stop this disease, how can we prevent this from reoccurring?

But a common desire for the patients, and even more for their friends and families, is the wish to know "why" a terrible accident or illness has occurred, what was the cause. I and the other chaplains are the ones in the "why?" business, and fortunately or unfortunately, when we did our jobs well, that question was one we knew we couldn't answer. We could only help people answer that question for themselves and accompany them on their journeys. I grew to understand that when people look for what they might have done to have caused their own suffering, in a certain odd way, it is sensible and self-protective. We all want to have a sense of order in the universe, to believe that we are not just at the mercy of random forces. The feeling of being powerless and out of control can be worse than the feeling of having caused our own suffering. If we caused it, then maybe somehow, we can "uncause" it.

In the story of Job, his friends, at first sympathetic, turn on him in his suffering. Since they are not the ones being afflicted, they only have the patience to be supportive for just so long. We are all perhaps at least a little guilty of this; we don't like to be reminded of our own vulnerability, of the mystery surrounding suffering, or feel powerless in the face of it. If our religion has taught us black and white answers to the "why?" questions, we feel uneasy in the territory that Job is in. Elaine Pagels, biblical scholar and professor of religion at Princeton University, who within the space of two years lost her six-year-old son to a congenital illness and her husband to a rock-climbing fall, says, "In times of grief the church has little to say. It's just too remote....You wonder, how can I cope? You wonder, whatever happened to a sense of proportion in the universe? But the universe, of course, is not about that. [My husband] had a sense of all this. His work [as a physicist] was all about chaos—chaos theory. But in me...there was a subliminal perception of a morally ordered universe." [Elaine Pagels, quoted by David Remnick, *The New Yorker*, April 3, 1999]

Job's friends suggest to him that his sufferings are the "discipline of the Almighty" (5:17). This is, unfortunately, a view of suffering that we are all too familiar with. "Blame the victim," it's called. The set-up of a conversation between God and Satan in which God seems to agree to the torment of Job just to make a point to Satan is an unappealing idea to us. But we are familiar with the view that tragedies are the work of Satan, of demonic forces. It is so hard to accept that suffering is just a part of life. We construct our daily lives as much as possible to remove any feeling of vulnerability.

We look to science and technology, to money and mobility, to solve every problem. But sometimes they fail us; sometimes we are confronted with how their misuse or our own partial knowledge has created more problems than we can solve. Sometimes, despite our best efforts, terrible things happen to us, to those we love. "It is God's will," often ends up being the catchall explanation for whatever we can't figure out. But while the idea of something horrible being "God's will" may solve one problem, it creates another. How can we love and feel close to a God who causes suffering? We don't even like the idea that God "permits" it.

When we or those we love are suffering, we may find ourselves very, very angry at God. And our religious training tells us that that is not OK at all. So, we don't express it directly. It's just not done. We try to pretend. Even though we know that we could not be intimate with people with whom we are not emotionally honest, we think we can lie to God, by being silent about our anger.

We go through the motions of a religious life, wondering why God seems so far away and remote.

We conclude that God is useless, that religion is unhelpful, merely a way of thinking leftover from a more primitive age. And then we wonder why we feel such emptiness. Far better for us to complain to God as Job does, for then we remain in the relationship. Then we can come to know the truth of the words of Jesus which we read this morning in Luke's Gospel, that by endurance we will gain our souls. We discover that our understanding and, even more, our acceptance of life as it is will deepen.

We might ask, but why does Job wish to be in a relationship with this God whom he believes to be tormenting him? Why should we? Why does Job not "curse God and die," as his wife suggests early on, turning away from the whole mess? But for Job to abandon his faith in God would be as a great a disruption in the fabric of his life as the terrible things that have happened to him have been.

Instead of giving in, he speaks up to God; he names God's behavior as unjust. Having lived as a devout man all of his life, he cannot imagine turning away, but he doesn't mince words about his outrage, saying in a parody of Psalm 8, "What are human beings, that you make so much of them, / that you set your mind on them, visit them every morning, test them every moment? / Will you not look away from me for a while, / let me alone until I swallow my spittle?" (7:17). He speaks up, he complains, but he also expresses his faith; no matter what happens, he believes that at the end of it all, he will see God.

The intention of the Book of Job is not to explain why people suffer, nor to justify "the ways of God with humanity." Rather, the intention of the book of Job is to explore the depths of faith in spite of suffering—the way in which a soul is gained. Job's faith is not a quiet, inward thing, but rather, a vital and alive relationship. This relationship is what is put to the test, and even though Job cries out against what is happening to him, he does not turn away from God nor from his belief in himself.

Job in his suffering comes to know God in a way far beyond what was possible for him when his life was smooth and easy. In his final response to God he says, "I had heard of you by the hearing of the ear / but now my eye sees you." Job has been changed from a man who believed in God because of the religious traditions of his day, a man with a complacent and unquestioned faith. Job has gained his soul.

We need one another while we struggle towards wholeness. The young need the strength and wisdom of the old; the old need the energy and optimism of the young. Those who have power need the searching openness of the powerless, and the powerless need the action of those with power. Those who mourn need to be comforted, those who are joyous need to share their celebration. We who make up this community called church need not to be silent in the face of grief, but to reach out to one another. Not because our words can instantly heal one another. Not because we can make it all OK so that no one ever has to feel bad again. But because we are in God together.

In the season of Advent, the season in which we anticipate once again the birth of Christ, Christ who came to us in Jesus of Nazareth, born as a helpless baby—who as well as knowing the joys of human life would suffer disappointments, griefs and losses, and who would die too young, on a cross. We could say that the world was already a sad old world when he came into it, and that it is sadder now. Or we could say that through him we see the marvelous depths, the wonderful colors and textures, the glory of the life that is given to us. We could call this our season of lengthening out, of going deeper.

Heinz Pagels, husband of Elaine, physicist and research scientist, who died in a rock-climbing fall, said in his book *The Cosmic Code*, written six years before his death, "I dreamed I was clutching at the face of a rock but it would not hold. Gravel gave way. I grasped for a shrub, but it pulled loose, and in cold terror I fell into the abyss. Suddenly I realized that my fall was relative; there was no bottom and no end. A feeling of pleasure overcame me. I realized that what I embody, the principle of life, cannot be destroyed. It is written into the cosmic code, the order of the universe. As I continued to fall in the dark void, embraced by the vault of the heavens, I sang to the beauty of the stars, and made my peace with the darkness."

Elisabeth Horwitt

The Fair Folk

"The Oregon Country Fair creates events and experiences that nourish the spirit, explore living artfully and authentically on earth and transform culture in magical, joyous and healthy ways."

Oregoncountryfair.org

"Path Rove: 'Fair Central? We've found our no-wristband friend. Sadly, he's gone up a tree. What should we do?'

Fair Central: 'Let our friend know that we aren't going to cut down the tree tonite, but we'll be sure to catch up with him later!'"

Famous and Favorite Fair Quotes

I first encountered Sweepers on the first day of the Fair. I'd just finished my afternoon shift at Bicoastal Grill and was eager to explore "the Eight," the Fair's main drag.

Every July, a small village springs up in a patch of woods in Veneta, Oregon: wooden booths selling tasty food and all kinds of original and handmade arts and crafts. My progress was slow, as I kept stopping to admire, touch, try on: a painted hawk mask, a tie-dyed skirt, a carved wood spirit, a "fresh-picked" hanging rainbow. There was a "Touch the Earth" booth that sold prayer flags and candle lanterns, and a "Touch the Sky Books" booth that sold journals and notebooks with covers of crafted leather and hand-painted paper.

It was almost closing time, and I walked among weary, sun-dazed tourists dragging their kids and backpacks towards the main gate. As I reached the crossroads (aka the Junction) where the two loops of the Eight meet, I heard jaunty, brassy music approaching from behind, and turned.

First came a crowd of weird, vivid creatures: birds with pink balloon plumage shook baggy, pink and orange behinds; giant mosquitoes poking their long proboscises at screaming children; a stately, leaf-crowned tree with a solemn face and twinkling eyes.

Up came the band, horns, and saxophones swinging, and a throng of dancers boogying to, of all things, "The Teddy Bear's Picnic."

If you go down to the woods today,
you're sure of a big surprise
If you go down to the woods today,
you'd better go in disguise.
'Cause every bear that ever there was
will gather there for certain
Because today's the day the teddy bears

have their picnic.

Behind the band came a line of people stretched across the path, their hands clasped to form a living barrier. They were all smiling and walking jauntily, as if they were having a wonderful time.

> *Every teddy bear who's been good*
> *is sure of a treat today*
> *There's lots of marvelous things to eat*
> *and wonderful games to play*

The band paused at the Junction, along with a crowd of gaudily dressed and painted dancers and a few tourists bopping along with the band. The human chain came up slowly from behind.

"Who are those people?" I asked a woman with glittery bare breasts and a gaudy stomach around which a hula-hoop undulated.

"Sweepers," she said. She glanced at my silver Mylar wristband. "You're okay, you're Fair Folk." Warmth spread through me. I was "with it," as the Carnies say. I belonged.

As the human chain approached, three teenagers broke out of the crowd and darted down the left side of the loop—only to run up against yet another smiling line. They tried to break through, but the clasped hands held firm. Sulkily, they rejoined the crowd of tourists, and the Sweepers resumed their jaunty march, herding them relentlessly towards the exit.

> *At 6 o'clock their mommies and daddies*
> *will take them home to bed*
> *Because they're tired little teddy bears.*

As the Sweepers approached me, I held up my wristband. The two nearest smiled and raised their arms. I ducked under and headed back down the Eight, feeling light, free, and slightly weirded out.

"I just met the Sweepers," I told my friend Peggi, who owned Bicoastal Grill.

"They didn't hassle you, did they?"

"Nope. I showed them my wristband. The Fair is pretty strict about security, isn't it?"

"You don't know the half of it." She told me that after they had finished herding the tourists, Sweepers scoured the Fairgrounds for outsiders, who hid in the workers' campgrounds and even climbed trees. I wondered why they were so determined to stay after closing.

I found out that night. As darkness fell, the booths lit up with strings of colored bulbs, Japanese lanterns, candles, and neon. Musicians sat in front of booths, playing folk, bluegrass, and Allman Brothers' songs on banjos and guitars, harmonicas and didgeridoos. Fair Folk in elaborate costumes wandered around, meeting friends and sampling each other's wares. The sweet smell of pot was in the air.

I ate a falafel sandwich and a brownie then followed the sound of thunder to the Drum Tower, where I joined an ecstatic crowd dancing to the pounding, percussive beat.

It was almost 2:00 a.m. when I crawled into bed. Bicoastal workers' tents are quite luxurious: a foam mattress, sheets, and a pillow, even a battery-powered lamp. Outside, the fair was still going full blast: yells and laughter, clang of steel drums, wail of a baby in the next tent. Fortunately, Peggi had warned me that the Fair was an all-night event, and I'd brought a white noise machine. I fell asleep to the soothing sound of crashing waves.

Next morning, I visited the Ritz, a beautiful structure of natural wood that contained a group coed shower, a sauna, and a fire pit where Fair Folk gathered

102

to talk, sing, and chant. At Blazing Salads, I ordered a bowl of oatmeal topped with yogurt and fresh berries. "Give that nice lady whatever she wants," the owner called to the server. "She's from Bicoastal!"

At the communal table, I chatted with a shaggy, bearded man who lived on a small island in Puget Sound and said he was homeless as a matter of principle. "I'm organizing all the children around the world to go on strike for peace," he said. If I'd been anywhere but there, I would have gulped my oatmeal and left fast.

I said, "Great, go for it."

The gates didn't open until 11 am, and the Eight was quiet and peaceful. I wandered up to Chela Mela Meadow, an open field with pavilions as brightly colored as the kites soaring in the air. People held up wands that streamed elongated, rainbow bubbles. Kids of all ages chased each other and practiced juggling and backflips.

Heading back for my 11:30 work shift, I was overtaken by a jostling crowd of tourists, newly released at the front gate. My peaceful, dreamy mood was punctured, and I felt invaded.

I ran into my son JP at the booth. "The Ecological Police were harassing us," he complained. They'd visited the teenagers' campground and told them they couldn't hang sheets on branches because it might kill the trees.

I admired the Fair for being so ecological—it runs entirely on biodiesel, for instance—but couldn't help thinking it sometimes went too far. There were six trash cans, one for just paper, another for plastic, a third for paper with food on it, and so on. By the end of the day, they generally contained six piles of mostly undifferentiated garbage.

As I set out metal containers of grated carrots, sprouts, and Caesar dressing, I wondered aloud why such a free-spirited, tie-dyed event as the Fair needed so many rules. "People who work here enter a contract to behave a certain way," replied Dave the Pookah, a fellow worker who wore gigantic rabbit ears and gave great massages. "Fair Folk are like family. There's no crime, and everybody helps each other out."

I remembered the free breakfast I'd gotten at Blazing Salads. And when Bicoastal ran out of lavash bread, the Whole Enchilada gave us two big boxes of tortillas. I remembered how peaceful and easy I'd felt walking down the Eight before the hordes arrived.

When my shift ended, I attended a Cris Williamson concert on the Main Stage then checked out booths on Shady Lane, the left-hand path of the lower Eight. Approaching the Junction, I caught up with the Sweepers and their reluctant captives. The band was playing "Sing, Sing, Sing," impossible not to dance to. A glittery woman on stilts matched her steps to mine, and we danced our way to the front gate, where the band struck up, "So long, been good to know you." We waved them out, then turned and wandered back along the Eight. Dusk was falling, and the faerie lights were coming on. Somewhere off to my right, notes of a flute rose like iridescent bubbles. I quickened my step, my heart thudding. The real Fair was about to start.

Dorothy Irwin

Years of High Hopes

Excerpt from *Years of High Hopes: A
Portrait of British Guiana 1952-1956,
from an American Family's Letters Home*

One snowy winter some time ago, I spent several weeks in my Brooklyn living room reading the letters my mother had sent fifty years earlier to her parents in the United States from Georgetown, British Guiana (now Guyana), where she and my father, Marian and Howard Irwin, lived from 1952 to 1956. My father was the first of several Americans to arrive by means of a Fulbright teaching grant at Queen's College, the colony's preeminent secondary school for boys. I was born in Georgetown toward the end of my family's stay. During those years, my mother wrote her parents at least once a week. In three and a half years, she composed 190 letters.

Reading the letters was slow going; some were handwritten in faded brown fountain pen; many others bore the faint typescript produced by a well-worn ribbon, and all were composed on onion skin that had for decades sat folded in envelopes now brittle with age. Sometimes, as I opened the paper, tiny swatches of fabric fell out, or a 1-inch-square snapshot, or a yellowed newspaper clipping. A direct link to another time, the letters that made up this cache of ephemera had been written when, other than costly telegrams, mail was still the sole form of overseas communication with British Guiana, a sugarcane colony considered part of the West Indies (and now, as Guyana, the only English-speaking nation in South America).

Beyond my interest in my parents' efforts to get their bearings in unfamiliar surroundings and make the most of their years in Georgetown, I was struck by the richness of life, Guyanese life, recorded on those pages. Then a year's worth of my father's letters to his parents surfaced. By virtue of his job and the greater mobility accorded to men, his accounts of goings-on around town (and well beyond) dramatically boosted the scope and level of detail.

Having lately taken an interest in my birthplace, I'd begun reading novels by Guyanese authors, when I could find them. But this correspondence wasn't fiction; real relationships and interactions are portrayed, some hilarious, some sobering, some of startling poignancy in the misunderstandings or vulnerabilities, conflict or courtesy they reveal. The letters spill over with the messy immediacy of real life. And, by sheer chance, they were written during a period of historic change: 1953 saw the colony's first free election and the surprising victory of its first modern political party, the People's Progressive Party, followed by the new legislators' brief term in office, which was brought to an abrupt end with the suspension of the constitution and the arrival of British troops. I was sure it was wrong for this extraordinary record of events large and small to remain unseen by anyone but the few of us who had written, received, or inherited it.

At the center of the letters is Queen's College. Founded in 1844 as a school for sons of the privileged, the college had by the 1950s opened its doors to working-class boys throughout the colony, boys who won places by qualifying for government-backed scholarships. Queen's had moved to new, modern quarters in 1951, and by then enrollment was up to 459, nearly triple that of twenty years earlier. Its roster of high-achieving alumni includes Cheddi Jagan, the country's first prime minister (and Guyana's president from 1992 until his death in 1997), and its first president, L.F.S. Burnham, both of whom were among the reform-minded legislators elected, and then ousted, in 1953.

When my parents arrived in the colony, they discovered that some foreign servants thought of it as a hardship post. Once flourishing, it was by 1950 poor, which meant that salaries were relatively low. Among the British, it had a reputation for backwardness. It was farther from England than any of the other Caribbean colonies, and its isolation from them was palpable. Yet among Guyanese, the early 1950s are sometimes looked back on as a golden age. In the postwar world, hopes ran high. The British Empire was breaking up, education and employment restrictions had been loosened; technical and medical advances had begun to improve daily life, and optimism about further, desperately needed changes took hold. But in the post-election fervor of 1953, those hopes started to be checked, and for decades an impassioned, contentious, often violent, and at times downright corrupt stalemate, influenced and sometimes backed by foreign interests, hampered efforts toward positive change. Today, long hobbled in its struggle to establish a cohesive national identity, Guyana's ongoing plight stems in no small part from what took place in the 1950s.

Sugar was British Guiana's economic mainspring. Workers who made their way out of the cane fields found limited opportunities. Well into the twentieth century, residents of Georgetown adhered to the "carefully structured, stylized constraints of life in a small colonial society," writes Noël Bacchus in *Guyana Farewell*, a memoir of his youth in British Guiana in the 1930s and 1940s. Bacchus's father had worked his way up in the civil service to become the registrar of deeds, the highest type of position to which black Guyanese could aspire. (Even in the 1950s, East Indians—the descendants of indentured laborers from India who, along with those from China and Portuguese Madeira, had been brought in after Emancipation to take on work formerly done by black slaves—held civil service posts only on an exceptional basis.) As the Guyanese novelist Roy Heath writes in his memoir, *Shadows Round the Moon*, the civil service "represented the ambitions of a class, which saw in it a guarantee of material security, a second-best when resources to study medicine, dentistry or law were lacking."

At Queen's College, boys of all backgrounds were brought together. Bacchus, who grew up in Georgetown, describes his first days at Queen's in 1947, when he encountered a number of "country boys" from outlying areas. "All we knew of each other was that most of us had won scholarships in the colony-wide, competitive examinations for admission," he writes. His previous six years of schooling had taken place in a single room, where reading and instruction occurred amid the din of recited lessons. "Something as simple as a separate

108

classroom was a novelty after the open space and clamor of elementary school," he writes. At Queen's, he says, he and the other boys found the facilities and the coaching that enabled them to specialize in the fields of their choice and compete professionally on the world stage. Matriculation was, for many, a life-altering achievement. Even to acquire a secondary education was a feat, as compulsory education in British Guiana was limited to primary grades; to have the chance of becoming something other than a laborer was a distinct advantage. For one boy (and one girl) per year with a truly distinguished scholastic aptitude, that might take the form of a government-paid scholarship to a university abroad.

The curriculum taught at Queen's—and at Bishops' High School, its counterpart for girls—focused on the Northern Hemisphere; it was keyed to the syllabuses of the Oxford and Cambridge Board intended for schools in Great Britain and used throughout the empire. "What is a birch, please, Miss?" Mona Williams asked her music mistress at Bishops' in the mid-1950s after learning a lyric in which the word appeared. "The lessons were fabulous and joyful, although they felt completely disconnected from my life," Williams recalls in her memoir, *Bishops*, where she also tells of being taught to cook with imported carrots, potatoes, cream, and beef, all too costly for local budgets.

Queen's reputation as an "elite" school cut both ways. Many Guyanese criticized its favoring of the humanities over the sciences, a bias that had the double effect of promoting British cultural values and keeping Guyanese unqualified for good positions. It was common practice in the colony to hire from abroad (at better salaries) any engineers, chemists, electricians, and mineralogists, and Queen's had not elected to help overturn that tradition to benefit locals. For the three years preceding my father's arrival, the school, lacking a biology master, had offered no biology classes at all, a particular hindrance to students who hoped to pursue careers in medicine.

This was the modest world in which my parents found themselves in September 1952. Its distance from their lives in the United States then was vast and from our more global consciousness today is practically immeasurable. As Bacchus writes, "The opportunities that we considered special in that small impoverished British colony seem, in retrospect, so limited and inconsequential that it is difficult to conceive how important they were to us, our families and the society."

Yet present-day Guyana makes no sense unless it is seen in the context of its past. My parents' letters are a portal to a moment that, however much it may still impinge on Guyana's progress, is no more, the character of its constraints, grievances, and small kindnesses nearly forgotten. Its evanescence is what makes the contents of this book so valuable.

Abigail Johnson

Women's Fight for Equal Rights Takes a Leap Forward

Counting down to the February Winter Olympics in Sochi, Russia, the media spotlight is shining on the world's best athletes. Some of them are women. A few women are ski jumpers.

This year, for the first time, women will be allowed to compete against each other in the ski jumping event. Sports aren't my passion (understatement.) I knew nothing about the contentious history of women's ski jumping until I heard a riveting report by Tamara Keith on NPR.

According to Keith, the International Olympic Committee (IOC) repeatedly told female jumpers their sport was not "at a high enough caliber" to qualify for inclusion in the Olympics, though women often soar as far or farther than men.

Women have competed in ski jump events for over 100 years, but the IOC had never recognized the event for women. Why the segregation? According to the

Women's Ski Jumping USA organization, "some considered that women's bodies couldn't handle the sport—not unlike what was said in the 1970s and 80s about women marathoners." And in the 1960s.

Kathrine Switzer, now 66, was the first woman to enter, run, and finish the men-only Boston Marathon in 1967. As recounted in this month's *Prevention Magazine*, "Wearing the race bib # 261, she was attacked by one of the organizers, and the assault was immortalized in photographs of that historic race." The anger and fear in the faces of men shoving Switzer evoked Civil Rights strife in the same decade. Switzer finished, determined to create opportunities for women to run. In 1972, women were welcomed in the Boston Marathon, and at the Olympics for the women's marathon.

In 2008, women ski jumpers from six countries sued for the right to compete in the 2010 winter games in Vancouver, B.C. The Canadian court ruled the IOC was practicing gender discrimination but did not force them to add the event in 2010. The next year, the IOC added one women's ski jumping event, called "normal hill competition" for the 2014 games. Men have three ski jumping events.

The IOC used women ski jumpers from past Olympics to, "make sure the ski jumps were safe for the men," according to NPR. I was chilled (excuse the pun) and horrified. I thought of the Tuskegee airmen, the patriotic African-American pilots who flew escort planes for heavy bombers in World War II piloted by whites. Or female WASP pilots in WWII who flew stateside missions to free up male pilots for overseas assignment but had no military status.

When Jessica Jerome and her teammates represent the United States in Olympic women's ski jumping, it will be a big leap for women's sports. Women are making strides—in marathons, on ski slopes, in society. For women to truly soar—and by that, I mean achieve and sustain equality—societies and cultures must embrace ability and competence, without discrimination. Based on the protracted struggle of women ski jumpers for Olympic recognition, women's equality continues to be earthbound and measured in small steps.

Carol Kindig Urbanic

Kirkland Reminiscences

I still call it Kirkland.

I'm writing up these reminiscences two weeks after my 40th reunion at Kirkland College while memories of a small, but fun and lively, get-together of the Class of 1976 are still fresh in my mind. When I did that math at the reunion last year, it seemed mind-boggling that I was so close to the number 40! I realize now how much I've changed from the introverted 17-year-old who applied early decision to Kirkland College back in the fall of 1971 during my senior year in France with what was then the American Field Service. Kirkland was definitely my first-choice college—from the moment I heard about this unusual new college that didn't have grades, a college for women that was coordinate with a men's college across the street. I still remember touring the campus with my Dad, driving around New York State, Pennsylvania, and New England over spring break in his Volkswagen Beetle. I vaguely recall having an interview in Admissions. But I can still remember investigating colorful dorm rooms and talking with some friendly Kirkland students, which probably tipped the balance for me.

Ah, Kirkland...its grey concrete buildings with almost brand-new furniture that went so well with the modern buildings. Waffle ceilings, brightly colored Venetian blinds, green trees, and apple blossoms.

The Kirkland campus has changed a great deal since I graduated in 1976, with buildings being renovated and added on to, especially the Kirner-Johnson Building, where I passed many an evening studying and writing because it was too noisy in the dorms. It is always bizarre to walk around that building at reunions—and I've attended several—because I know where I am in space. But some things are missing—like the spiral staircase—and things have been added, like chairs in the Red Pit. The KJ Auditorium (which we sometimes called the "Purple Pit") has also been updated and brought into the 21st century. Many of you probably remember going to the movies there on weekends for a dollar in the 1970's. We would watch classic old movies such as *It Happened One Night*, not to mention Fred Astaire/Ginger Rogers movies, funny Marx Brothers films, and many more.

Not being a city girl, I was quite easily entertained at Kirkland, in my rare moments of spare time. I remember lingering over meals at McEwen on occasion and having long and deep conversations with my girlfriends in our lounges, or while sitting on the floor in the halls of the dorms. I recall listening to live music at the old coffee house and drinking that ghastly Russian Tea, which was primarily warm Tang with spices! For those under 40, the Tang of that era was fake, powdered orange juice, supposedly drunk by American astronauts.

Other memories, which I imagine many of my classmates might share, were getting warm raisin bread from a bakery down in the Village of Clinton, enjoying the woods, the sunsets over what were then empty fields, and the beautiful flowering trees in the springtime. I remember Hamilton in the fall but Kirkland in the winter and spring most strikingly.

Another vivid memory was having an early dinner in McEwen on weekdays, finishing by 6:00 p.m., so I could treat myself to an hour of the original *Star Trek* reruns with a bunch of friends before heading off to homework. Kirkland was a huge challenge for me—heavy amounts of reading, lots and lots of writing (on my second-hand, blue electric typewriter, which in 1972 didn't have an automatic carriage return—hard to imagine now!), and participating in class with Kirkland and Hamilton students who were much smarter than I thought I was. I was "stretched" by my classmates and by my professors. Rather than competing for A's as I did in high school, I came to compete with myself. For four decades, I've told people that the detailed, constructive Kirkland evaluations meant more to me than my grades in previous schools ever did. I still have the evaluations in a box in my closet.

Kirkland was stimulating, both in and out of the classroom, because of my classmates and my professors. Words fail me now—there is so much I would like to say, but it is impossible to condense my feelings into a sentence or two. Suffice it to say that I am who I am today in large measure because of Kirkland and my Kirkland mentors. I often felt sorry for my children, both of whom attended large universities and whose professors barely knew them, at least for the most part. They used to be shocked when I would tell them that my biggest non-lecture class at Kirkland was 28 people, and even that one split in two for a once-a-week discussion class. As I wrote in a piece I submitted to the "Kirkland Pioneer" project a few years ago, Kirkland's emphasis on writing, personal growth, responsibility, and service made it a unique institution.

Over the years, many people at Hamilton College have informed me that there is a great deal of Kirkland in today's Hamilton, helping to make it the top-notch institution it has become. I take comfort in that now. In the early years after Kirkland vanished, I was devastated, bitter, and even angry. It hurt that my college—which had been such a huge part of my coming of age—no longer existed and that no other young women would have the advantage of attending the college and enjoying its benefits.

I've mellowed over the years, but for me, it is always bittersweet to return to the campus. I have come to accept it all though, or most of it, because I believe there IS a sizable remnant of the college I once attended. This remnant exists not only in the buildings—however changed they are—but also in the Kirkland professors for whom the Hamilton administration was wise enough to grant tenure back in the 1970's. They of course left their mark on Hamilton, injecting some new energy and ideas into that older institution. The remnant is also present in several programs in which Kirkland had been strong, such as the arts, creative writing, and independent and cross-disciplinary studies, but also in, for lack of a better word I am going to call, Kirkland Spirit.

This spirit was evident at a recent All-Kirkland Reunion, out of which has grown an active movement to help Kirkland alumnae help and mentor current Hamilton women, and perhaps to host a summer program to be called the "Kirkland Institute." I tremendously admired the energy of all these Kirkland women—an almost palpable energy. Many of these women came back for the first time since graduation, overcoming at least some of the negative feelings they had for decades, in order to figure out how they can give back to our alma mater.

It's still Kirkland.

One thing that has been so special for me about the Hamilton/Kirkland reunions all these years later is that I feel I can go up and strike up a conversation with anyone with a green name tag—even the "Pioneer Women" (that is, Kirkland's charter class)—knowing we Kirkland women were and are all part of a very select group, a sisterhood. In the words of Natalie Babbitt, who years ago autographed one of her books for me with the line, "because we shared Kirkland," it's the shared experience of a college that no longer exists in name, but is still very much alive.

I too am a Kirkland Pioneer; I'm a part of the Kirkland legacy.

It's still Kirkland College because of the people, the life we shared at Kirkland, and our special vision for taking charge of our own growth and education.

Kathryn E. Livingston

Role Reversal: When the Kids Are the Grownups

I'll never forget the day I dropped my middle son off at college. He was my "easy" child, and I was having a really tough time as he'd decided to go to a university six hours from home. (My other two boys attended nearby colleges, so the separation wasn't quite as dramatic.)

As I stood sobbing outside my car in the parking garage after we'd unloaded his belongings and attended all the first-day-at-college/separation events, Sam pulled a Lifesaver out of his pocket. "Want a candy?" he asked, giving me a big, rib-cracking hug.

"Whoa!" I thought to myself, tearfully accepting his offering. Total role reversal. Isn't offering a treat and a hug supposed to go the other way around? In addition to the angst caused by the fact that my son was leaving home was this new twist: it was possibly the first time it seemed like *he* was the grown-up and I was the kid.

Not long after, I was practicing my yoga handstand against the front door (the only free wall in my cluttered house) when my eldest son (who works in the computer world in Manhattan) happened by. "Stop that!" he admonished. "You might hurt yourself!"

Hmm, those words had a familiar ring. It sounded like something I might have said when this same young man was a child diving headfirst down a slide or climbing a tree in the backyard.

There's probably a point in every parent's life when our kids start telling us how to behave. Suddenly, the children who were once so busy with their peers and activities, their jobs or their studies, look at us and realize we, the parents, are doing some mighty foolish things and they had better warn us. In fact, I remember telling my own aging mom that she had better stop drinking soda (which she loved) and eat more kale (which she detested). I probably made my mother's advancing years rather miserable with all my instructions and directions. Actually, I think I was a lot bossier with her in her old age than she ever was with me when I was a child.

Once I started noticing this new phenomenon with my sons, I got a little freaked out. My kids thought my husband and I were "crazy" to be driving a 13-hour stretch when we recently went down south to visit my sister (who at 70 is just starting a new career). "Have a safe trip," Sam said, calling me on my cell during our voyage, "and be careful; there might be snow when you go over the mountains!"

Be careful of the snow? Since when, I wondered, do my kids tell *me* to be careful? Not long after, I went to the mall with my youngest son, a college senior. He grabbed my elbow as we negotiated the parking lot and warned, "Watch out for cars!"

Now, hey, let me be clear, I am not a doddering old woman. I am a pretty fit yogini who can do an inversion with aplomb. So why the heck, I wondered, are my boys treating me like an octogenarian (never mind that their grandmother on their father's side *is* an octogenarian who still does yoga, drives, works, and travels)?

At first, I was amused. Then baffled. Then, I guess, a little insulted. Until I thought back to my own mom and remembered that the reason I started bossing her around was just because I cared about her and fervently hoped that she would live forever.

So, I guess I should cut my kids a break. Okay, so they think I'm a little too old to be driving from New Jersey to North Carolina in one day, a little too old to be placing my hands on the floor and flipping my body up against the front door, a little too elderly to be packing a tent and heading to New Mexico on a yoga retreat.

I'm happy that they care; actually, I'm quite touched. But it is payback time, and I don't intend to be any less naughty than they once were.

Anne Mavor

I Am My White Ancestors

Excerpt from *What Does it Mean to be White in America: Breaking the White Code of Silence, a Collection of Personal Narratives*

There hangs in our hallway matching portraits of my great-great-grandparents, Eugenia and John Buchanan, photographed around 1860 in Orangeburg, South Carolina. Eugenia sits in a chair with one hand on her lap and the other draped over the edge of a table, lace at her throat and wrists. She is pretty with ringlets hanging down on either side of her perfect oval face. John has fierce eyes and black unruly hair. The story passed down was that they were Confederate spies.

I've had these photos for about ten years, ever since my parents died. I also brought home transcripts of my grandmother's taped recollections about her family in South Carolina since I remembered my father saying that she had talked about some of the plantations her extended family owned before the war. At the time I didn't even read the pages, just jammed them into a box with the photos to send home. I had a feeling that someday I would need this information.

Growing up there had been no mention of plantations in the family or enslaved African people working on them. It was a given, I guess. There but not referred to, like the large cannonball in the front yard of the house in Orangeburg where my grandmother grew up. The information didn't even need to be repressed because it wasn't brought up in the first place. In our family, confronting each other and asking uncomfortable questions was just not done. But I had questions. How was I similar to my ancestors? Would I have acted any different? What were they thinking? But I felt embarrassed about my curiosity, so it sat waiting.

In the fall of 2013, I had just completed a series of paintings of ancient stone circles and mounds in Britain— my attempt to connect with the land of my ancestors. While casting around for my next step, I came up with the idea of inviting a Native American artist to collaborate on a project comparing our relationships to our sacred sites. But a few days later, I realized what I was doing. Like many well-meaning white people, I had side-stepped my own heritage and instead was using a person of color to legitimize my artwork. So, I asked myself, "What if I turned it around completely? What if I claimed my own people instead and took responsibility for their actions? What would that look like?"

Images of Eugenia and John floated before my eyes, along with my grandmother's memories and the boxes of photos and letters sitting in my sister's basement. The individual lives of my family clearly fit into the American and European story of racism, colonization, genocide, and class. Could I use my history to examine the source of those oppressions and model what taking responsibility might look like?

As if it was a gift from the cosmos, a project materialized in my mind. I would research and choose 12 ancestors, 6 men and 6 women, who represented the range of oppressive actions committed during European and American history. I would create costumes, paint backdrops, and photograph myself as those characters. The portraits would be life-size and displayed together in an installation. And the ancestors would tell their conflicting and dramatic stories through audio diaries. The title: I Am My White Ancestors.

Then the doubts began to crowd in. Could I really do this? What would it take? How long? How would I fund it? Create the costumes and paint the backdrops? Record audio diaries? Who am I kidding? But among those thoughts was the knowledge that within my family history lay the seeds of racism, and I wanted to reveal them, whatever it took.

I began with Eugenia since I had her photo and a good amount of information about her. In addition to my grandmother's taped recollections, I used letters and a book about Eugenia's escapades during the war. The story about them being Confederate spies turned out not to be exactly true, although John did have to escape to Mexico with a price on his head during General Sherman's March at the end of the Civil War.

As I reflected on her life, I was hit with a new understanding of my family legacy. The characteristics before me were all so familiar: obedience, separation, ignorance, and quiet endurance. Following her husband all over the south to avoid the northern aggressors. Leaving her baby daughter behind in South Carolina with her sister Lou. Watching Union soldiers burn down the

124

family home. Not understanding why her remaining enslaved Africans didn't want to travel with her on to Chappell Hill, a bastion of South Carolina Confederates in eastern Texas. Finally, joining her husband in Mexico where they spent 10 years trying and failing to start a sugar cane plantation.

After six months of research, I ended up with characters covering 2000 years of European American history from 1870 back to 300 BCE. In America, the list includes two slaveholders from South Carolina and a pilgrim from Plymouth Colony who gained land and resources from the Wampanoag. Traveling back in time to Britain, I chose a Scottish farmer who was a juror on a witch trial, an English mercenary soldier and social climber who fought to colonize Ireland, and an English noblewoman caught in the middle of the bloody War of the Roses. In the medieval era, there is a Basel cheesemaker, who supported the execution of Jews during the Black Death; King Edward I of England who conquered Wales, invaded Scotland, and expelled the Jews from England; and a Frankish countess who became a nun and benefitted from the colonization of Jerusalem during the Crusades. Lastly, I found a Norman knight who helped Duke William conquer England, a female Viking who invaded Orkney, and a gold metalworker from the Celtic Iron Age who supported the warrior elite.

In choosing the ancestors, I looked for individuals in each century who were involved in carrying out oppressive actions against other people and who I could show were also oppressed or hurt in some way. It was important to make them real and complex enough so that white people, in particular, could identify with their choices. As a white person living in the 21st century, I still carry all those stories and beliefs in me, though they may be disguised or invisible, at least to other white people.

It has been easier for me to understand and identify with the female characters since I share the experience of being a wife and mother. On the other hand, Sir Nicholas Baganel is not someone I want to know. Born in Staffordshire, England, in 1510, he fled to Ireland after being accused of murder in a pub brawl. Known as a ruthless warrior, he was employed by Henry VIII and Elizabeth I in their efforts to keep the Irish down. In addition to scorched earth tactics and battles, English soldiers and their Irish collaborators rounded up migratory Irish into plantations. Baganel must have learned early that violence is admirable, and the Irish are expendable. It reminds me of the genocidal treatment towards Native Americans that began 100 years later.

My assumption when I began the research was that oppressive beliefs and behaviors like racism, colonization, and genocide had their source in Europe. We must have learned them somewhere. Patterns like greed, arrogance, superiority, and believing that conquering other people and their land and resources is the right thing to do, in the name of honor, religion, family, and country. I was not proven wrong. All are illustrated in European history over and over.

The most personal part of the project has been acknowledging that I came from these specific people. My body is connected to them, the color of my skin, the shape of my nose and eyes, the texture of my hair, my height, my hands, all of it. That is why the act of physically embodying my ancestors has been so important. For the photoshoots, I put on types of clothes they might have worn and imagine my hands fingering a sword, wielding an ax, carrying a bowl of soup, skinning a rabbit, sewing a dress, preparing for the next battle—believing that I am right.

One more story. My ancestor Desire Howland Gorham was born 1623 in Plymouth Colony. Her husband, Captain John Gorham, fought and died in King Phillip's War, the last stand of the Narragansett Nation and their allies against the English. Following this war, all captive Indian males were enslaved, sent to the West Indies, and their tribal lands distributed to the English soldiers, including the Gorhams. However, any Indian servants who were already employed by English settlers could remain with their employers. In one of the genealogical books, I found references to an Indian servant named Tooto who worked for Desire. In his will dated 22 December 1691, Tooto asked to be "buried as near his mistress's feet as may conveniently be" and left two oxen to pay for his burial. He then gave his possessions to Desire's children and grandchildren.

I always want to cry at this point in the story. How could he be so generous to people who had destroyed his culture? I want to believe that Tooto was a cherished person to this family, crossing the social and ethnic barriers. More likely, he had been removed from his family as a child and didn't have anyone else for whom to leave his possessions. Even so, I want to believe that, given a chance, human connection always wins out.

Embracing white identity and heritage as a step towards ending racism might seem counterintuitive. But this history is living in all white people in varying ways, and the more we deny it, the bigger it looms. For me, this process has been a way to understand and feel a part of my historical family, while at the same time taking responsibility for their actions and the privileges I inherited.

Patricia McLaughlin Amidon

Cruising the Great Loop

Hannah escaped almost certain starvation when at the age of eighteen she ventured up the gangplank of the sailing ship docked at County Cork and bound for North America. The time was the early 1870s during one of the direst Irish potato famines. I know little else about my great-grandmother but am very aware that her willingness to step into the void, to risk the unknown, to take the road less traveled is very much alive in me, particularly now that I am retired.

I first became aware of the Great Loop just about eight years ago when my husband, Bob, and, I along with two other couples, chartered a boat to explore the Erie Canal for a week. During this trip, we learned the canal is but one short segment of the Great Loop, an extended counterclockwise boat trip that circumnavigates the eastern half of the United States and portions of Canada. When Bob found this out, I could see the wheels in his mind turning at full speed.

As someone who almost drowned at the impressionable age of nine, the idea of a long water voyage was not a high priority on my to-do list. Bob, on the other hand, as someone who spent every childhood summer sailing and swimming, considered the Great Loop a can't-pass-up adventure. Herein lies the nature of our relationship. We are the ultimate "opposites attract" couple.

Our marriage has been punctuated by a great deal of head butting. He votes one way, I the other, so our votes typically cancel each other out. He is the thesis, I, the antithesis, and as the chart plotter was up and running again, we left Portsmouth and headed to the Isles of Shoals off the New Hampshire coast where we picked up a mooring for the night. The next day, while cruising to Boston Harbor, the rear head ceased to function. We both thought that perhaps this adventure was cursed but didn't say anything to the other.

The head issue took several days and a plumber's snake to repair. It was an unpleasant task; the details are too disgusting to share. Suffice it to say, we were elated when that problem was solved. We naively thought that after this crisis, nothing more could possibly go wrong. We continued our journey, leaving Boston behind only to discover that the bow thruster which was just replaced before we left stopped thrusting. We only cruised as far as Hingham Shipyard Marina where the boat needed to be hauled out the first time to diagnose the problem, parts were ordered, and the boat was hauled a second time to correct the problem. Another week passed. We were now into August. The window of opportunity to cruise up the Hudson River, out the Erie Canal, into the Great Lakes and enter the river system at Chicago by mid-September had slammed shut.

Lesser mortals would have caved, but not this Kirkland pioneer and her intrepid spouse. We persevered. Why rush, we asked ourselves. Let's head south and start the Great Loop from some point in Florida in the spring. We spent the remainder of August cruising Long Island Sound, the months of September and October in the Chesapeake Bay where we enjoyed the 200th anniversary of the writing of the "Star-Spangled Banner" in Baltimore on September 14, 2014, and visited Washington, DC, by boat. November found us cruising down the Intercoastal Waterway through the Carolinas and Georgia. December and January found us enjoying the warmth of the Florida sun.

On January 27, 2015, Velo-Mer left the dock at Stock Island Marina Village in Key West and headed north on the official start of our Great Loop adventure, retracing our steps up the east coast to New York City. We spent the first week in June moored at Sheepshead Bay in Brooklyn, enjoying the culinary delights of the area. We cruised north up the Hudson River, passing West Point to Waterford, New York, where we turned to our port to enter the Erie Canal westward-bound through 25 locks, stopping briefly in Utica to visit with another Kirkland graduate, Dolores Mancuso Chainey ('72). From Erie, we entered Lake Ontario and cruised to the Bay of Quinte and the Trent-Severn Canal through 44 locks to Georgian Bay, the North Channel, and Lake Michigan to Chicago. At Chicago we entered the river system, dodging commercial barge traffic, eventually arriving at Mobile, Alabama, on the coast of the Gulf of Mexico, and cruised eastward along the Florida panhandle. We made an overnight passage from Carrabelle on the panhandle to Tarpon Springs on Florida's west coast, returning to Stock Island Marina, Key West, on December 15, 2015.

The Great Loop took ten and a half months to complete. We cruised 6,515 miles, put 800 hours on the engine, consumed 1,520 gallons of diesel fuel, and spent

114 days cruising. Other than an emergency root canal at Annapolis, Maryland, the impenetrable fog off the New Jersey coast, going hard aground on the Trent-Severn Canal in Campbellford, Ontario, between Locks 13 and 14 which delayed us four weeks for extensive damage repair, raging eight-foot seas in Georgian Bay, and being caught in a terrifying lightning storm on Lake Michigan, we experienced a phenomenal voyage.

This was an adventure that literally changed our lives. We were challenged and stretched to our limits, we were brought to the brink and back again, we learned to work as a team like never before. We benefited from the kindness of strangers and the embracing camaraderie of fellow loopers; we learned about the War of Northern Aggression and others' historical perspectives that differed from what we learned in school. We learned geography; we learned to read the wind and the water; we encountered amazing wildlife including looking eye to eye with a dolphin racing alongside Velo-Mer. I learned how to change the oil and filters in a diesel engine. Every day taught us something new both about ourselves and about the world around us.

On the evening of December 15, as we sat on Velo-Mer's flybridge enjoying an adult beverage and congratulating ourselves on not only surviving but also thriving on the Great Loop, we both felt this impending void entering our lives. All the exciting plans we had made for post-loop life somehow seemed totally irrelevant. A land life no longer fit our psyches. We looked at each other and said in unison, "Let's keep cruising." Finally, we totally agreed on something! Europe can wait.

Helen Morse

The Centerline

Debbie was an adorable child, with blond ringlets, skinny legs, and knobby knees, always festooned with Band-Aids from adventures gone slightly wrong. She had big dimples on either side of her mouth, like our father, and hazel eyes in a striking honey gold color. She loved roughhousing and anything physical, and never quite took to my sedate interest in playing with dolls. She was happiest on the swing set in the backyard, pumping her legs to achieve lofty heights, or hanging from the strong vines of the Banyan tree nearby, pretending to be Tarzan.

Debbie was younger than me by two years. We shared a bedroom from the time I was four or five until I turned ten or so. Carolyn had just been born, and she stayed in Greg's (the governess's) room for all of the nighttime feedings and general care of an infant. In our room, there was an imaginary line down the center. Debbie had drawn it out. She liked to have control of things, and this was just one example. It was easier to go along with her plan than to try and change it. I was her big sister, but I was generally more tractable, and it was clear that Debbie needed control, even at this young age. This "centerline" existed in many other areas of our relationship and Debbie's general interactions with the world. I simply accepted that this was her way. She needed to be the boss, and being older myself, it simply didn't mean as much to me most of the time. Later on, I protested when my mother shared with me that I was her favorite, but I silently carried that burden of guilt for Debbie's sake, which colored all the interactions I had with her forever afterward.

My sister had been born with a chip on her shoulder, but from my young point of view, she'd earned it. Mom always blamed her for causing her kidney problems, as Debbie had "sat on them" during her whole pregnancy. It was also Debbie's birth that had coincided with my mother's hearing problems. She never lost an opportunity to remind Deb of this in the many years to come. Debbie felt her outsider status acutely. She was always being compared to me. And it never went well. It was always, "Look, Helen is dancing, go dance with her." Then there would be giggles at her sweet and childish attempts to imitate me, accompanied by not-so-quiet whispers about Debbie's less than swanlike delivery. It was, "Look at Helen's drawing, isn't it wonderful? Let her show you how to do it." My parents appreciated my skills, while athletic prowess, one of Debbie's skills, didn't interest them. I was the pretty and talented little girly girl; Carolyn was the amusing and adorable baby; Debbie was the inscrutable and defiant tomboy. Our roles were cast early, our value as members of the family too.

Thus, she was overseer of the goings-on in our bedroom. The toys and closet with more toys were on her side, the bathroom was on mine. Whenever I wanted a toy, I would have to wait until she needed to use the bathroom. This resulted, as planned, in my having little to do but sit on my twin bed and wait, playing with whatever toy was already on my side, until she broke down and had to go. She made a point of waiting as long as she could, tickled by the idea that I had to wait to claim a new amusement. "Don't you need to use the bathroom yet?" I'd wheedle, clearly pained by the desire to get another toy. "Nope," she'd say, grinning her devilish grin. She had no interest in the baby dolls or tea set I possessed that resided on her side. Her preference was for the stuffed animals and blocks and games that filled our room. I simply complied. I had to wait to gain access to them, as these were the rules. There was tremendous humor in this, which we both recognized, to be sure, along with a slight flavor of retribution, which I accepted as fair. Debbie was the boss, and that was that, as long as Greg was occupied elsewhere and wasn't there to intervene.

When we played games outside, Debbie laid down the ground rules. Whether it was tag, hide and seek, or Marco Polo, we went by Debbie's rules, no matter how we protested. Even when the rules were stacked in her favor, and they often were, complaints were shrugged off. As we grew, this mode of interaction never changed.

During typical sibling scuffles, if she felt I had gotten the upper hand, she would pinch herself until it left a mark, and then run to our mother saying I had done it. While I got the prodigious spanking, Debbie would crouch somewhere within sight and smile at me. The mark was proof enough for my mother, and I was beside myself with remorse, not for having done anything, but for allowing my sister to put me in this situation.

She could be fiercely protective too. From her very beginnings, she stood up for what she felt was right.

Once, when we were quite small, she and I had been out in front of the house when a neighbor boy approached us. I was around eight, and she had to be about six, the same age as the boy approaching. The boy had flame-red hair and a face so full of freckles that there were no breaks in the pattern. He was somewhere between Debbie and me in height and was sporting a baseball jacket covered in insignias of all descriptions, lending him a kind of tough guy aspect, at least to us at the time. The boy spoke, addressing me, "Do you know what I'm going to do with you? I'm going to tie you up and throw you in our motorboat and drive you out into the middle of the lake and throw you in!" His eyes were on fire to match his hair, and I was duly impressed and frightened. At the moment when he'd managed to take my breath away and I was verging on tears, Debbie, much smaller than him, replied, "Oh, no, you won't!" and socked him solidly in the solar plexus, turning on her heel as the boy crumpled onto the pavement. I followed along, her wimpy big sister, grateful and proud of her guts in the face of such a threat.

When she was at her best, she was funny. She had a wry sense of humor mixed with a devilish grin that made us all laugh. She loved to stir the pot, declaring with some regularity that one or another was cheating at a board game, often just for the rise she would get. She loved games of all kinds, Mousetrap, Monopoly, Yahtzee, and cards, which never failed to raise her spirits. Competition was her comfort zone. As a pre-teen, Mad Libs were a great favorite, and she never failed to think up the best and most appropriately appalling words to fill in when asked for a noun or verb. At times like these, her laugh was hearty and unreserved. As she got older, she never lost that appreciation for bawdy jokes and black humor. I always made sure to send her a funny card on the holidays as she didn't appreciate the sentimental stuff as much.

She was very territorial. When we were teens, it was Debbie who could demand the most unbelievable gifts at Christmas. One year, Debbie asked for a Sunfish, a small sailboat, to use on the intercoastal waterway! To our amazement, Santa delivered. Debbie would not allow either of us to use it. Her territorial nature forbade any such activities when it came to things she valued. She never used it beyond the first few days of possession, and still, she would not loan it out. It was a peculiar kind of selfishness, which she never viewed as anything more than what was right and fair. We had our stuff. She had hers. Ownership was all.

Above all things, Debbie loved animals. Aside from our family dog and a parakeet, and various gerbils and fish, she had her own personal pet, a cat she'd discovered living in the neighborhood who had no owner. It was a lanky and underfed creature with dirty, longish fur in mixed tones of black, gray, and brown. Every day for months, she lured the cat in with treats and bowls of food until it finally allowed Debbie to pet its long coat. From there, with more food and incredible patience, she was able to pick the cat up and bring her indoors. Debbie named her Toto, and they became fast friends. No one else could befriend Toto. True to form, Debbie would not allow it, and as the cat was already skittish, the cat remained hers and hers alone. For most of the time, Toto lived outside, doing what she liked, going where she wished. When Debbie was home, all she needed to do was call to her, and she would magically appear out of the greenery, ready to greet and spend time with her friend. By then, her general appearance had improved remarkably, and she was obviously grateful for Debbie's ministrations. She allowed Debbie to brush and fuss over her in every way. Toto even took to delivering mice in a neat line to our side door for Debbie; a tribute to their closeness. At dinnertime, she would take Toto back outside, where Toto preferred to be. It was around then that Debbie confessed to me that she liked animals better than people. I could not blame her, even as her actions often pushed others away.

Debbie had a horror of her first baby picture. She often compared it to mine. I had been born with a full head of hair, and the picture of me was of a child who had a mild and not unpleasant expression. Carolyn's too was mild and sweet. By contrast, Debbie's photograph was of a completely bald baby, not unusual, as she was a very blond child, but the photographer had caught her at an unfortunate moment in which she appeared to be gazing down at something very scary just out of view. Her eyes were open wide and staring, while the baldness added to the impression Debbie described as the enormous cranium of an alien. She hated the unflattering picture, but seemed to be drawn to it. I recall many times she would bring it up as proof of the fact that she was different. I was never quite sure why. I did not blame her feelings about it, although I did my best to reassure her that it was just a bad picture, not some indication of anything else. Debbie never relented on this point, and I suspect it was because she was trying in her way to express something more troublesome.

There was something else. The bad photo aside, there was something different about Debbie. She was extremely willful and could be selfish, to be sure. She was also shy with strangers. She was territorial and could be almost tyrannical with Carolyn and me. But those things didn't describe it either. It was that Debbie was never really joyful. She took small difficulties harder, and the good things were always less so. I knew it then, but could not have put words to it. The problem wasn't only the family we were born into. I knew where our family had left its scars. But this could not explain it all. Carolyn and I found ways to find moments of happiness, even in the household as it was. It is a coping skill that we all must devise, no matter our situation, for survival's sake. As far back as I can recall, I have no memory of Debbie ever expressing true happiness at anything. She kept virtually everyone but Toto at arm's length and was never quite satisfied, no matter what. She showed great gleefulness at winning any kind of competition, yes, but it was not the kind of happiness that comes with feeling good within one's own skin or with solid contentment among one's fellows. Back then, as her older sister by only two years, I could not say how I knew that there was something wrong with Debbie, but I knew it the way you know the sky is blue. You just know.

Ellen J. O'Brien

Re-empowering Rhetoric: Performing Language-driven Plays in a Language-deaf Culture

Language in Shakespeare's plays is an active, dynamic force. Moving on the gears of rhetoric and meter, it opens the gates of Harfleur, enables Richard II to uncrown himself, and, from the mouth of Queen Margaret, brings doom on everyone in sight. This dynamism is not simply a theatrical effect: it is the manifestation of a cultural attitude toward language in general, and rhetoric in specific.

Language in our time has become expression rather than action, a vehicle rather than an agent. For us, physical actions (and images) speak louder than words. Rhetoric is often a dirty word; curses and oaths have been nearly drained of their power. Our fundamental problem in speaking Shakespeare's language is not the words that we do not understand nor, in themselves, the rhetorical tropes and figures that we miss. These are surface details.

A deeper problem stems from the fact that we neither think *about* language as Shakespeare and his contemporaries did nor think and feel *through* language as they did. Even when the words are familiar, we may not understand the language culture from which they spring. Without that understanding, actors may resort to driving the language rather than allowing the language to drive the character and the action. Thus, they are often forced to drag the plays along paths where language once drove them like a mighty engine.

How do we perform Shakespeare's language-driven plays in a culture where language is rarely perceived as having inherent force, where curses, oaths, and vows have all but lost their active power, where political rhetoric has declined into buzzwords and subtextual emotional appeals, and where "you know what I meant" constantly privileges sub-text over text? How do we train actors to make the language of these plays accessible to an audience whose expectations are shaped by such a culture—to make accessible not simply the meaning of these words but the dynamics of the language, its force and energy? Can we enable them to harness not only the power of word and image but the power inherent in the structural dynamics of the language—and to do so in a way that speaks to audiences of our time by opening their ears to what they do not yet know how to hear? Perhaps the first step is to come to grips with the nature of some key differences between Renaissance and 21st-century language.

I. Rhetorical Theory: Renaissance and Modern

Today, we tend to think of rhetoric as essentially decorative. At worst, we think of it as empty language— full of sound and fury, signifying nothing. But for the

140

Renaissance, these tropes and figures were the manifestations of "habits of thought and...methods of developing a thought" (M. Joseph, 3.) Integrally linked to logic, rhetoric was far more than a decorative art: it implied ways of thinking and modes of argument very different from our own. Consequently, if we are to activate more than a small part of the potentiality of Shakespeare's language, we need to grapple with his culture's modes of thought and argument, not simply with the externals of figures and tropes.

We also need to recognize that while rhetoric is "artificial" to both modern and Renaissance minds, those minds mean something quite different by the term. To us, something "artificial" has no basis in nature, is at best a poor imitation of nature, as in "artificial vanilla." To the Renaissance, all artifice has its roots in nature. Witness Sir Philip Sidney in his "Apologies for Poetrie":

> There is no Arte delivered to mankinde that hath not the workes of Nature for his prinicipall object, without which they could not consist, and on which they so depend, as they become Actors and Players, as it were, of what Nature will have set foorth. So doth the Astronomer looke upon the starres, and, by that he seeth, setteth downe what order Nature hath taken therein....The Grammarian speaketh onely of the rules of speech; and the Rethorician and Logitian, considering what in Nature will soonest prove and perswade, thereon give artificial rules. (Smith 1:155)

Thus, what is creation *ex nihilo* to us was a revelation of fundamental truths of nature to the Renaissance. Rhetorical structure (properly employed) was not something layered onto the thing spoken, but a natural form for the thing spoken to take.

Given these contrasting attitudes toward rhetoric, it should be no surprise that rhetoric no longer occupies the central role in education that it held in the Renaissance[3]. As a result, our actors and audiences are far less grounded in rhetoric. But even more important than our lack of familiarity with rhetoric is the fact that rhetorical theory has changed radically in a number of ways which are in themselves reflections of shifts in the broader culture. "It is the business of rhetoric to react to the situation in which it is used and to reflect in its theory the needs that it serves" (Howell, 160-161). Our rhetoric reflects and serves our own time; it can also obstruct our access to Shakespeare's rhetoric—and hence to the dynamics of his plays.

In his "Renaissance Rhetoric and Modern Rhetoric: A Study in Change," Wilbur Samuel Howell identifies "five changes in the ancient theory of communication [which] began to appear during the Renaissance and by and large...help to explain why modern rhetoric is as it is." Four of the five are important to the actor's encounter with Shakespearean language, but the first—a breakdown of the alliance between logic and rhetoric—may have the most profound impact[4].

Despite differences of opinion on their precise relationship, logic and rhetoric clearly entered the

---

[3] For details of Renaissance education, *see* Baldwin and Miriam Joseph.

[4] The other three changes are: a shift in invention toward emphasis on external realities; a shift in "the method of arranging ideas for public presentation" from the complex to the simple; and a shift in style from the "artful and elaborate" toward the language of ordinary speech.

Renaissance as profoundly interconnected disciplines. Today, Howell declares, "rhetoric has lost its productive association with logic" because "logic has dissolved its alliance with the communication arts and has aligned itself instead with the theory of scientific investigation." As a result, the "fragments of logic" which still appear in rhetorical treatises "have not represented the full emphasis of the new logic and usually, indeed, have been conspicuous for their perfunctory character, their lack of originality and their seeming dedication to the appearances rather than the essentials of the tradition they reflect." Meanwhile, logic has "denied the priority of the syllogism, and has politely sought to disavow those who wanted to use the study of logic as a practical means of making themselves logical writers and speakers."

When rhetoric and logic are perceived as integrally related, rhetoric functions as thought in action. A part of the dynamic of argument and proof, it operates on both the intellect and the emotions. Conversely, once divorced from logic, rhetoric becomes mere presentation, "as in the elocutionary movement of the nineteenth century, where rhetoric became completely absorbed in delivery, not in the Baconian sense of the full act of communication but as the vocal and physical components of that act." The separation of logic and rhetoric therefore means that we don't hear rhetoric as an active thought process or mode of argument. We are not trained to hear structure as a form of proof, much less to assess the validity with which the rhetorical structure is offered as proof.

In addition, although the 19th-century form of elocution may have been admired in its own time, it has left rhetoric a heritage of suspicion. As long as rhetoric was linked to logic, its impact was both emotional and intellectual. Divorced from logic, rhetoric became almost entirely emotional in its impact, and in our time, emotional manipulation has become suspect (though hardly inoperative). "Mere rhetoric" has come to be a standard term for empty language, particularly the political. To a significant degree, rhetoric seems not merely dissociated from logic but the enemy of logic, a set of tricks used to obscure the facts rather than to reveal them. Thus, for modern actors and audiences, the very presence of rhetoric may seem to signal the likelihood of deception or manipulation. This is not, of course, to claim that no one in Shakespeare's plays uses rhetoric deceptively, only to assert that a Renaissance audience would be given to making distinctions between legitimate and illegitimate uses rather than to suspecting rhetoric in general. As a result, abuses would strike a deeper chord. When actors learn to make that distinction, they are one step closer to effectively engaging Shakespeare's rhetoric.

Excerpted from: "Re-empowering Rhetoric: Performing Language-driven Plays in a Language-deaf Culture." *The Voice and Speech Review,* 2005. After discussing other changes in Rhetoric which create obstacles to 21st-century actors, the essay posits some approaches to integrating Renaissance Rhetoric into current actor training.

Works Cited

Baldwin, T.W. *William Shakespeare's Small Latine and Lesse* Greek, Urbana: 1944.

Howell, Wilbur Samuel. *Poetics, Rhetoric, and Logic: Studies in the Basic Disciplines of Criticism*. Ithaca: Cornell University Press, 1975. 140-162.

Joseph, Bertram. *Acting Shakespeare*. N.Y.: Theatre Arts Books, 1969.

Joseph, Miriam. *Rhetoric in Shakespeare's Time*. N.Y.: Harcourt, Brace and World, Inc. 1962.

Pole, J.R. "The Language of American Presidents." *The State of the Language*. Ed. Leonard Michaels and Christopher Ricks. Berkeley: University of California Press, 1980. 421-431.

Shirley, Frances A. *Swearing and Perjury in Shakespeare's Plays*. London: 1979.

Smith, G. Gregory. *Elizabethan Critical Essays* (London, 1904), 1:155.

Wilson, Thomas. "Arte of Rhetoric," qtd. in *The Art of Rhetoric*. ed. G. H. Mair. Oxford, 1909, 160.

Gwynn O'Gara

A Room That Grows

The room I named my studyo is upstairs in our house. It's where I read, write, think, practice yoga, and keep track of earnings and expenditures. Over 23 years I've assembled journals, books, feathers, stones, shells, family photos, jewelry, art, broadsides, and bouquets living and dry. At the east window sit file cabinets and two desks, one with my computer, the other with an inbox; a day bed and a bookcase share the west window. Bookshelves line the walls; a couple of rugs, chairs, and tables hold more books, acorns, seaweed, et alia. This studio, library, laboratory, launching pad, office, gallery, and getaway invites me to experiment, invent, and cultivate peace, clarity, joy, ease, and the fallow state that sometimes precedes creativity.

Before my husband, son, and I moved to the edge of this small town 23 years ago, my need for a solitary workspace was met by the diminutive dining room of our tiny San Francisco apartment. While on a business call during the 6.9 earthquake of '89, I sheltered under my desk as the world shook and shook and shook. (The man

146

I was interviewing tried for days to reach me to learn that I was safe.) Under the chandelier I'd recently inherited from my mother, I also worked on poems and stories. When our son was born the following year, my study became the nursery and I moved to a desk in the living room. No matter how my room changes, it always holds me; I just need to recognize its sometimes-invisible walls.

My current room is off our kitchen under a severely slanted southern roof that limits half the room's length to short people and low bookshelves. Windows at both ends bring in dawn and dusk, trees and traffic. To let in more light and air I crank open two screened and shaded skylights. On broiling summer days, despite the fan I place beside me, the space becomes uninhabitable, so I descend to the below-ground playroom that I'm slowly turning into my library. But on summer nights my studyo's a tunnel of cricket song, pulsing so palpably it vibrates through the bones of my head. Pacific wind regularly sweeps through and fog doses me with minerals and messages. Winter rain drumming on the skylights gets intense. Proximity to the kitchen allows bursts of focus during dinner prep, which has kept me sane over the years but can detract from my cooking.

Along the high wall, my husband and I built a gap in the bookshelves, where I hung a Mexican mirror festooned with snakes and flowers. Because of the abundant light, it's where I put on makeup and brush and braid my hair. Gradually an eclectic altar's grown up around the mirror with photos of my mother and grandmother, father and brother, statues of Guadalupe, Buddha, a Taoist holding a tea cup, a Navajo Grandmother Doll cradling a baby, a straw Rice Goddess, frogs, fossils, angels...

147

I didn't have to fight for this room, but others before me did. After a youth of relocations and losses, and during the stress of the early years of marriage and motherhood, my room served as a healing haven, and I give thanks every day for how it continues to nourish and root me.

As a child I was answerable to anybody but myself, mostly to my mother and the nuns at school, who trained me to be an extravert and sacrifice my needs and wants for their comfort. (The nuns get the blame for indoctrinating me with a grim God that allows true happiness only after we die.) As with many women, it took me years to grow up, develop a strong ego, and find the magic balance of loving self and loving others. Not only did my room help me discover I'm an introvert, it also helped me create *roomth*, an obsolete Old English word meaning "sufficient space." Good word, *roomth*.

I named my room my studyo because this is where I study and dance. I read poems and books about birds and butterflies, stars and trees, how to grow pomegranates, and when to harvest runner beans. A few mornings a week I unroll my mat and explore asana, chanting, breath, and mudra. Some evenings I unwind onto my back and catch up with my breath, or sprawl on the rug and read. Sometimes I just need to be on the floor, as when after the birth of our son, my milk came in and I buried my face in our three-flight walk-up's carpeted floor. I cherish a floor of my own as much as a roof, windows, walls, and a door that I can close.

In yoga, we work toward spaciousness in body, mind, and heart, and the consciousness that we are connected to everything and that within each of us shines a sorrowless light. Creating room for release and movement, awareness and emptiness, we observe thoughts and feelings along with pain and delight. Of the many ancestors of the modern word "room," most named a space, but a few meant scope and opportunity, the way that we make room for ourselves in the house of the world. Another root meant the hold of a ship, which protects our stores and treasures through powerful seas between harbors. Indeed, our gifts can carry us through life and often provide safe passage.

Over the years I've come to understand that we have a room of our own inside ourselves, in the space we open within, through the process Keats called soul-making. Poems and phrases, moments of intense feeling and perception, lessons learned, ideas, people I love, including strangers, alive and dead, fill my inner space, which is also my memory palace, hut in the woods, and mountain home. The walls are porous and protean.

My studyo's energy field extends to our garden, which we cultivate for bees and hummers as well as humans, with fresh water for birds, plants that nourish with food, beauty, color, scent, butterflies, and fruit. I feel deep-down pleasure feeding others as well as ourselves. My brother jokes that we've created our own "temperate zone," where when we're not working our butts off, we relax and feel free.

Down the road the teeming eco-system of the 50-acre ranch-turned-park also inspires awe and astonishment, tranquility and inspiration. In the overgrown heart of the old ranch under ancient oak trees, I tend a wild azalea overrun with blackberry switches. The oak grove does not belong to me; it's a room in the commons, for everyone. My inner room overlaps with it, and I'm grateful they're still growing.

Jo Pitkin

Letter by Letter

Words. From the moment I arrived in Iowa City, Iowa, in 1979, I was utterly focused on words. Although I was the second youngest in my Workshop class, I was a veteran of workshops. A graduate of Kirkland College, I belonged to the first generation of undergraduates who received a bachelor's degree in Creative Writing. My college poetry teachers Tess Gallagher and Michael Burkard were themselves Workshop graduates, so I felt thoroughly prepared for graduate school. Nonetheless, I had not yet broken the poem down to examine its essential, elemental parts.

While attending the University of Iowa's MFA program, I had the privilege of studying poetry with a number of teachers, including Donald Justice, Jane Cooper, Larry Levis, and Sandra McPherson. After a poetry workshop, Sandy once took me aside and advised me, "Don't let them take your words." I understood what she meant. She wanted me to hold on to my particular vocabulary despite the fact that plain, unadorned language in poetry was the fashion at the time. Still, it was vaguely thrilling to imagine a thief lurking in the shadows, poised to steal away my words. This implied to me—a twenty-three-year-old woman—that my words had value. I began to grasp that words should be guarded and protected. And they could be owned—and wielded.

In Justice's incomparable and renowned Form of Poetry class, Don demonstrated how to dissect words. We listened very closely, and we broke words down into their syllables and accents. Words, then, had an interior skeleton of sounds, beats, phonemes. How precious and fragile words now seemed! They could be reduced to murmurs and sighs.

While in graduate school, I was fortunate to have a part-time job. Every day, I got up around 6:00 a.m. and took the city bus to Coralville. As an editorial assistant at The Riverside Publishing (then a subsidiary of Houghton Mifflin Company and its test publishing division), I cut my teeth on the editorial process: editing, copyediting, proofreading. Here, I learned the currency of words. I discovered that I could make money simply by moving words around, by reshaping them, by correcting them, by marking them with a red pencil.

Outside of the Workshop, I took Introduction to Typography with Kay Amert and learned how to set metal type by hand and use a hand-operated letterpress. Although I had founded, edited, and produced my college's literary magazine *Red Weather* with photo composition and an X-acto knife, Kay made type come alive to me in a more profound way. Not only were Bodoni, Baskerville, and Garamond the names of typefaces—they were the names of real men: Giambattista Bodoni, John Baskerville, and Claude Garamond. Long before the Center of the Book came into existence at the University of Iowa, Kay mesmerized us with fascinating stories about the men (at the time I wondered, "Did women design type?") who were obsessed with making letters look their best on a page, who sought to make words both readable and works of art. By the end of the semester, I had designed and typeset a broadside of my own poems, *Almost Home*. Through this arduous process, I found that my own small words became part of the stream of typographic history.

In another semester, I did an independent study with Kim Merker at Windhover Press. Every week, I went to a dimly lit workshop in the bowels of the English-Philosophy Building and set type. Standing in front of a California job case, I selected and lifted long gray metal bars with raised letters from small wooden compartments. A job case has its own specific arrangement, which you learn in much the same way you learn the arrangement of letters on a typewriter's or computer's keyboard. Each of its compartments held particular lowercase or capital letters, punctuation marks, or spacers. I spent hours alone, quietly and patiently lifting one letter at a time out of its jumbled nest and placing it in a line of type. Letter by letter, I built words. Words, I learned, had a physical shape and a metallic smell and feel.

This painstaking process of typesetting was both relaxing and rewarding. At the end of a class period, I could literally see progress as I set a few more lines of Windhover's next book—Samuel Taylor Coleridge's *The Rime of the Ancient Mariner*. Years later, I still remember the euphoria of watching a line of verse unfold. Yet it seems to me now that all of my Iowa teachers taught in their own ways a similar lesson: the sheer joy of making something letter by letter. Today, this process is inexorably linked to how I construct my poems, how I write educational materials for kindergarten through twelfth-grade students across the nation, and how I teach writing. When I taught my first writing class for college freshmen, I found myself echoing Sandy's advice to my own students: "I want you to value words," I told them. "I want you to value your *own* words."

At Iowa, I learned the power of the word. From many perspectives, I learned to respect words and treat them with care. It didn't matter what method I used to render them. Throughout the years, I have typed words on manual, Smith Corona, and IBM Selectric typewriters. I have set them by hand and with a Compugraphic photocompositor. I have processed them on PCs and Macs. Words have value. They have heft, texture, dimension, weight, shape. As Workshop founder Paul Engle said, "Poetry is boned with ideas, nerved and blooded with emotions, all held together by the delicate, tough skin of words."

Joanne Rappaport

Participation and the Work of the Imagination: a Colombian Retrospective (excerpt)

In the first edition in 2001 of the *Handbook of Action Research*, Colombian sociologist Orlando Fals Borda penned an impassioned appeal for the future of participatory research. Highlighting the importance of empathetic engagement, he identifies participatory action researchers (PAR) and the communities they work with as *sentipensantes* (thinking-feeling persons). He implores researchers to combine different types of knowledge through the collective exercise of a series of investigative techniques, framed by a research paradigm aimed at lending support to popular struggles. In the process, he argues, the attitudes of external researchers, as well as grassroots participants, will be transformed.

PAR as conceptualized by Fals Borda combined the rigorous collection of archival and oral materials with keen ethnographic observation in combination with a participatory process whereby local community organizations played a crucial role in determining research agendas and were the primary recipients of the results of research, which they would subsequently appropriate as political tools. But Fals Borda did not adhere exclusively to the data that he and his collaborators so meticulously collected. A vital component of the sort of observation he advocated was what I would call the "work of the imagination." Early PAR was typified by methodologies that engaged both external researchers and internal activists in an active process of imagining: envisaging scenarios for local history, crafting historical narrative out of stored objects, and identifying themselves in the history of their organization, thus effectively constructing alternative epistemologies through dialogic research practice.

The academic definition of research as a process of collection and analysis of data is only one way of understanding the research process. In contrast, grassroots participants in collaborative or participatory projects embrace research as a process of communal self-reflection. The combination of academic and grassroots notions of research into a single process entails, therefore, the bridging of substantial methodological, conceptual, and epistemological disparities, involving a dialogue between distinct knowledge-bases (*diálogo de saberes*) that encompasses not only their contents but also their form. Arriving at this common language involves not so much a process of reconciliation or compromise, as it does taking advantage of the confrontation between not-entirely compatible world-views, which, in clashing, produce knowledge. This process requires the work of the imagination, just as much as it presupposes diverse definitions of observable fact, dissimilar understandings of what constitutes rigor, and different approaches to and sources of theory.

Fals Borda's experiments in PAR emerged at an extraordinary activist moment in Latin American social science. Most recognizable to scholars and activists are the efforts by Mexican anthropologists like Guillermo Bonfíl Batalla and Rodolfo Stavenhagen to decolonize their discipline and the immense social impact of Paulo Freire's critique of mainstream education and his posing of a politicizing alternative in his *Pedagogy of the Oppressed*. Not as familiar will be the creation of the Rosca de Investigación y Acción Social (Circle of Research and Social Action), an action-research collective that Fals Borda founded with a group of other social scientists and journalists who were prepared to abandon academic life for a deeper commitment to popular struggles.

The reconstruction of history was a collective process that sought to create a new research model premised on the intellectual exchange between equals in the service of social change. They attempted to achieve this in various locations in Colombia, in particular, in the Caribbean coastal department of Córdoba in collaboration with the National Association of Peasant Users (ANUC) and in the southwestern highlands of the department of Cauca in concert with the Regional Indigenous Council of Cauca (CRIC). Both regions were hotbeds of alternative politics: in Córdoba a radical wing of ANUC appeared on the political scene, intent on occupying hacienda lands in the face of ineffective agrarian reform.

The construction of a revisionist history was central to La Rosca's objectives. Víctor Daniel Bonilla, who spearheaded the work of historical recovery in Cauca, intended his efforts in collaboration with CRIC to affect a break with existing discourses that saw indigenous

156

people as people without history. What is central to this project is a pair of linked objectives: first, the fostering of a process of self-conscious historical recovery within indigenous communities, and second, the contextualization of this process of historical interpretation within the broader history of the Colombian nation. In the process, communities would become capable of using their own historical vision as a tool for interpreting their place in regional and national society, and for recognizing their historical trajectory was intimately bound up into that of Colombia. Bonilla described this as a "rethinking of the relationship between the two societies" with the indigenous internal vision in the driver's seat. This recognition of the fact that researchers and local indigenous activists were fellow citizens marked, on the one hand, a step toward de-exoticizing indigenous subjects in social science research and on the other, a recognition that the two could be linked in a common struggle.

La Rosca's 1972 manifesto, *Causa Popular, Ciencia Popular* (Popular Cause, Popular Science), advocated a series of innovative methodologies blending research with activism. First, the research collective promoted an approach they called "critical recovery," which sought to unearth memories of grassroots institutions that had proven key to the success of popular struggles in the past. In Córdoba, extensive interviewing and workshops with ANUC leaders and grassroots organizations led to a revival of the "bastion of peasant self-sufficiency" (or *baluarte*), a politically autonomous entity governing haciendas occupied by peasant activists. The *baluarte* was an idea recovered from the memory of socialist struggles in the 1920s against the debt-peonage system; research on *baluartes* was encouraged by Juana Julia Guzmán, who led the first *baluarte* in the 1920s and collaborated as a narrator and ANUC firebrand in the 1970s.

These memories were reactivated through a process of "systematic devolution" accomplished through workshops, courses for local leaders, and the production and publication of pamphlets aimed at empowering grassroots organizations to take control of their future by recalling successful political strategies of the past and by situating these strategies in broader regional and national historical struggles that were taking place at the time. La Rosca activists in Cauca produced picture-maps condensing the major moments in indigenous political history, situating them in the topography of the region and resulting in mural-like cartographies that could be read and embellished on by indigenous activists in their native language. In Córdoba, La Rosca authored a series of graphic histories that contain illustrations peopled by historical actors in whom peasant readers could recognize themselves. As Víctor Negrete, one of the leading activist-researchers who worked with Fals Borda in Córdoba, observes in an interview I conducted with him, these pamphlets capture the style and tone of peasant narratives: "the work...is written to be read aloud; its writing style is *similar to* that of the peasants who were interviewed; its language is simple, characteristic [of the region], and a bit literary." Matilde Eljach, a student-collaborator of Fals Borda's, told me that the peasants "were moved when they saw their history in pictures" and began to sense that "they were the protagonists of...history." The graphic histories thus aroused strong political sentiments, which was one of La Rosca's aims.

The combination of rigorous historical research with innovative means of making it accessible to the grassroots unfolded thanks to the introduction of a series of techniques that were politically effective because they engaged the imagination of both external researchers and local activists, forcing them to think outside the box of official history and to adapt strategies for accessing local epistemologies. One of these was the collective perusal of the documents and objects saved by individuals in their homes. The contents of these personal treasure-troves not only motivated researchers to compose written materials in a language accessible to peasants but also allowed them to situate oral memory within a local historicity, one with its own distinct narrative arc and landmarks of memory.

In *Historia doble de la Costa* (Double History of the Coast), a four-volume work that recounts La Rosca's experience on the Caribbean coast against the backdrop of the history of land tenure and peasant struggle in the region, Fals Borda employs a technique he calls *imputación*, involving the rendering in creative literary form of the products of his research. For instance, when Fals Borda recounts the visit of a historical figure to a particular locale, he paints a verbal portrait of the place and includes imaginary dialogue, as though he were present at that distant event. In other words, he uses his historical imagination to depict scenarios and to render peasant narratives in accessible and pleasing prose, sometimes combining several narrators into a single voice, a technique he says he learned from Latin American novelists like Gabriel García Márquez (with whom he briefly collaborated, founding an influential leftist magazine, *Alternativa*).

At first, I suspected that *imputación* was a literary strategy that Fals Borda employed to render his historical narrative more accessible to readers. However, I later discovered that he advocated *imputación* as a technique to be employed in the field, in collaboration with local activists. The import of this technique becomes readily apparent in the panels of the graphic histories produced by La Rosca in Córdoba. *Imputación* was a strategy that situated historical interpretation in its oral, communal context, a way of simulating orality in writing. This was attained through the depiction of familiar faces in the graphic histories, many times represented both as historical actors and as aged narrators. It was also achieved through the portrayal of scenes of political action and of repression by the police and the hacienda-owners, complete with minimalist dialogue. These scenes had to be condensed and imagined out of the dense narratives that were shared at community meetings and captured, first in comic book drawings and only later in comic strips. The process of construction of the graphic histories was entirely collaborative: an interlinked series of interventions by peasant narrators, urban artists and activists, and the ANUC leadership, which supervised the process at every point in its production.

Since Fals Borda's time, PAR has entered into vogue within mainstream institutions; it is now a mainstay of World Bank and AID projects. But its appearance in the 1970s was considerably more creative and more inclusive—radical not only in its political stance but in its openness to collaboration. Today, when universities are slowly drifting toward neoliberal and corporate agendas, encouraging scholars to stop asking hard questions, Fals Borda's experience is a valuable reminder of the potential that innovative scholarship holds for social change.

Douglas Raybeck

Sensitizing Others to Cultural Bias

"The unexamined life is not worth living."
—Socrates at his trial

Whether giving public lectures, participating in the media, or simply teaching, most anthropologists tend, despite their well-known unhappiness with missionaries, to proselytize. We are usually interested in reducing prejudices, simple stereotypes, and ethnocentrism, but the means we employ in pursuit of this goal are highly variable. Probably, the most important avenue for us to achieve our ends of improving cross-cultural understanding is teaching, simply because we have the opportunity to work with an audience for a protracted period. One-shot lectures or radio commentaries are often quickly forgotten, but it is possible to reach students in a fashion that can be more lasting. I can claim no particular expertise in reducing ethnocentrism, but I have come across some stratagems that seem reasonably effective.

Students often approach anthropology either ignorant of its content or persuaded that they will be exposed to the primitive and the exotic. This latter expectation allows an instructor to encourage students to become aware of some of their cultural filters and to re-evaluate several of their own preconceptions and biases.

One of my favorite techniques is to encourage students to revel in just how strange are the practices of 'others' and then to bring home to them that what appear to be contrasts are actually similarities. In the past, a number of Northwest Coast Native Americans exchanged and even destroyed significant amounts of foodstuffs and materials. Thus, potlatches appear superficially to involve conspicuous waste. Certainly, several economists argued this in the fifties. Once we have discussed several articles on the potlatch, it can be useful to ask how many students have attended weddings costing in excess of $50,000. Thus far, the record is in the vicinity of $500,000 and makes the point quite nicely...even splendidly. Parents who spend that kind of money are seeking status, prestige, acceptance, powerful networks, and a column in *The New York Times*. They are far more likely to view their expenditures as a reasoned investment, rather than a frivolous waste, not unlike the Northwest Coast tribes mentioned above.

Again, rather than lecturing students on sociocultural similarities, it is useful to place them in contexts where they make the connection themselves. For instance, in teaching Chagnon's very popular text on the Yanomamö (1997), I ask students to describe their behavior at parties. Since Chagnon has been kind enough to supply both pictorial and verbal images of people drinking to excess, vomiting, and then returning to drink still more, this topic often surfaces in discussion. I can then ask the class if anyone could imagine engaging in such a strange and primitive practice. Nervous laughter indicates that most make the transparent connection between this ritual and the binge drinking they engage in on weekends (and, increasingly, on weekdays). Exotic perhaps, but neither primitive in origin nor in expression.

While behavioral practices are fun to skewer, examinations of belief systems can be even more telling and more useful for encouraging students to question their susceptibility to cultural baggage. Thus, readings and discussion of magical beliefs can lead students to the perception that such are characteristic of simple societies and unsophisticated minds. I then ask for the hands of those engaged in competitive sports and, once they are identified, ask how many have participated in or witnessed "magical practices" designed to ensure good luck and victory. There are numerous stories told of "lucky" items or behaviors, though the most extreme and complex are generally attributed to "someone else." I note that, as Malinowski (1948) argued, participation in such practices increases confidence and makes success more, not less, likely.

We then move on to discuss exam-taking practices and I describe a study of 250 students at SUNY Albany where it was found that forty percent used *special* techniques, clothing, or items to ensure success on exams. It is usually the case that a sizable minority of my students confess to having a practice or possession that brings "luck" to such engagements.

Similarly, students can often take the position that strongly held beliefs in the supernatural, whether these be magical or religious, are not characteristic of sophisticated thinkers, but are instead the province of primitives and prelates. After demonstrating just how hard it is to falsify a belief in magic (a ceremonial specialist zigged when they should have zagged, an unanticipated spirit was offended, the ingredients for the charm were impure, etc.), I ask for a student who has taken chemistry to volunteer for a "thought" experiment. I then suggest that they are taking a lab in which the object is to heat and combine two liquids in order to obtain a blue precipitant. I suggest that after they have followed the procedures described in the lab manual, they fail to get a blue precipitant, and then ask them what they would do. Students immediately say to repeat the experiment and, after I suggest another failure of the procedure, they then begin to supply a variety of possible remedies: replace the experimental apparatus, wash everything twice, change the chemicals for new ones, and so on. After this has resulted in failure after failure, I ask them at just what point they would assume that they had falsified the laws of chemistry. They get the point. I also find it useful to discuss the difference between faith in science, scientism, and the skeptical attitude that characterizes science itself.

The objective of all these exercises is the same: to make students less secure in their own convictions, and more sensitive to the beliefs and practices that they, often unknowingly, possess. I don't ask them to abandon their beliefs, but being conscious of them is the first step to being able to question and evaluate

164

them. Those beliefs that are retained are the product of an "examined life."

Bibliography

Chagnon, Napoleon (1997). *Yanomamö.* New York: Holt, Rinehart, and Winston.

Malinowski, Bronislaw (1948). *Magic, Science, and Religion.* New York: Doubleday Anchor Books.

William Rosenfeld

From *Margaret Tuger: The Extraordinary Teacher, Principal, and Community Leader of Herkimer, New York*

Several years ago, I organized a writing club that included residents of retirement homes in Oneida County. I assigned topics in advance of each weekly meeting, to which the participants brought their written responses. One week I asked the members to write about a school teacher or principal who had had an unusually strong influence on their development. As an example, I told them about Miss Tuger, especially her influence on citizens of the Herkimer community, its pupils, parents, pastors, and civil leaders. I assumed that communities other than Herkimer had had their equivalents of Margaret Tuger.

The outcome was surprising. Although my participants had settled into their retirement communities from all over the United States—many of them had worked in other countries—they assured me that none had ever known Miss Tuger's equal. To a person, she was one of a kind. So, I feel safe in asserting that she would have been outstanding in any setting.

In that spirit, I offer this with respect and affection, to the memory of Margaret E. Tuger.

Personal Experience

Here I present four of my own personal accounts. Each of them caused much embarrassment to me. That is my purpose for including them, for that embarrassment prompted my intention to get the record about Miss Tuger straight.

The first incident took place after I had moved up from Tuger School to North School—Herkimer's Junior High. The second is a conversation with two old friends during a visit to Herkimer. The third is a conversation during my last visit with my brother, Nate, then near the end of his life. The fourth occurred during one of Miss Tuger's visits to our home.

Miss Judson's Circus

One special feature of the move to North School was that students had a different teacher for each subject. Miss Judson's subject was Geography, and she presented an educational program each year, a sort of excursion and circus combination. All the continents were represented by posters, pictures of national products, and students in costumes appropriate to the countries they represented.

During the year in which I participated, Miss Judson fitted a paper mask to my face, put me in brown tights, and assigned me the role of "free-roving, monkey-ambassador." As such I was given liberty to caper, twirl, and skitter anywhere I chose on the gymnasium floor. It was an assignment I took to with gusto. I rode my knuckles and toes in side-steps, twists, cartwheels, from left to right and somersaults forward and back until...

Until Miss Tuger appeared at the edge of the gymnasium, waiting to intercept me in South America. She bent toward me with a nickel between her thumb and forefinger.

A confusion of reactions crowded my mind. Here was the personage whom I had always held in austere respect and, yes, let me admit it, fear. As I approached her, I wondered, how could I accept her into my clownish capers in front of all my fellow pupils? In one part of my mind, I could hear them yelling, "Take it! Take the nickel!" In another part, I heard them warning me, "Don't take it." In another, I heard myself saying, "If you take it, you must give her a kiss in return!"

But in writing this account I am left with both embarrassment and regret. I did not take the shining coin. Neither did I kiss Miss Tuger's cheek.

What would it have cost me? Nothing. In fact, I would have been five cents richer, and at the peak of the Depression, I knew the nickel's worth at the local soda fountain. But how could I, a made-up monkey, represent all Miss Tuger's children, her proxy family?

Well, as I say, I did not take the nickel. Instead, I turned a backwards somersault, executed a few twirls, and scurried away to another margin of the gymnasium.

I wondered what my refusal meant. A rejection of Miss Tuger's offer? Embarrassment to both of us in front of the entire assembly? The disappointment of the audience of students, teachers, other administrators? Which was it?

Angelo Lavallo's Barbershop

The second experience in this series of embarrassments occurred several years later. I was visiting my parents and, as usual, I stopped at Angelo Lavallo's for a haircut and to catch up on local developments. Angelo kept up with everything that went on in Herkimer. At one point, Cappy Casselle came in. I was happy he joined us because I had always admired Cappy for his emotional restraint and strength of character. After he took a seat, the conversation turned to the old days.

Angelo asked me, "Say, Bill, do you remember Miss Tuger?" Cappy shifted forward in his chair.

Without pause, "Remember her?" I replied. "Who could ever forget that marvelous figure?"

Angelo and Cappy went rigid in their silence. I had drawn a curtain between us. I realized immediately that I had chosen the wrong word, and I should have corrected myself immediately: "Wait a minute," I should have said, "figure is not the right word. I meant public figure, personage, presence." I wanted to make it clear that I meant something more respectful. Certainly not Miss Tuger's physique. After all, who would have dared be so familiar or informal in referring to that august personage whose memory called up such high respect and, let me say it again, awe.

Well, I didn't adjust my diction right then and there. I merely froze. My mistake was so shocking that I could think of no way to correct it by taking it back in favor of a more appropriate expression than Miss Tuger's figure.

Cappy, no doubt as embarrassed as I was, got up and left. Finally, with subdued goodbyes, I, too, left. We all three felt the chasm that had formed between us. That is the second blunder I referred to. It was entirely of my making, and I knew that sooner or later I would have to correct it, attempt to put into appropriate words my accurate recollections of Miss Tuger. It would be no easy task, for, unfortunately, my embarrassment did not end there.

A Visit with My Brother Nate

This is the third instance of my embarrassing gaffs. My wife, children, and I were visiting Nate, then very ill, in his home near Washington, DC. Our conversation wandered over several topics, but his last question to me was, "Bill, do you remember Miss Tuger?"

"Of course," I answered, "and how about Old Faithful?"

"Oh, well, yes, Old Faithful," he said, but dismissed my reference to the paddle and instead went on to recall the several ways Miss Tuger influenced our lives for the better—our respect for learning, our manners, deportment, respect for our parents, our patriotism. She was truly like an additional parent to us, reinforcing the encouragements our father and mother gave us. More important than anything, he had chosen her as a final topic of importance between us.

A Visit from Miss Tuger

I remember in particular and with considerable shame, however, the time my brother bawled me out for another of my several gaffs. Miss Tuger was visiting our home and during the dinner conversation, she asked me how I was progressing in one subject or another.

"Oh, fine," I answered, "because I remember a lot of what I learned at South School." That, I thought, was a fitting complement, but she leaned toward me with a look more tolerant than I deserved, and corrected me: "You mean Tuger School!"

I blanched and replied in a whisper, "Yes, Miss Tuger."

After she had left, Nate took me aside and asked, "How could you make such a mistake?"

I took his admonishment without reply or complaint. I knew he was right. To this day I shudder when I recall the incident.

Deborah Ross

Diana Ross Is My Sister

When the movie *Dreamgirls* came out ten years ago, I took my daughter, Violet, to see it. She was eleven at the time, loved to sing and dance, and like most girls had plans to become a pop star. Raven, it was then, about to switch to Miley Cyrus. As we were coming out of the theater, blown away by the music, she looked up at me with her big blue eyes and asked, "Do you think I could ever sing like that?"

Now we all know the right answer to this—it's an American standard: "Of course, you can be whatever you want if you try hard enough." I even opened my mouth to say these encouraging words, but they got stuck on the way out. Why?

Violet's question had brought me back to my own childhood—though in a sense, watching a movie that was sort of about the Supremes, I was already there. When "Stop in the Name of Love" came out in 1965, I was eleven, and I can still recall singing it on the porch with my friend Carolyn, working out the hand gestures, arguing over who got to be Diana Ross. I'm sure we were

172

aware that neither of us looked the part. We'd seen the Supremes lip-synching their hit on *American Bandstand*; that's how we knew to put up our right hands for the word "Stop!" Still, privileged little white girls that we were, the whole world was open to our fantasies, and that included Motown.

I recall arguing with Carolyn that I should get to be lead because my last name was Ross, but I knew it was useless. Carolyn had the prettier voice, the prettier face, and almost all the adult attention wherever we went. I felt destined to be her back-up for life, not realizing that being a better arguer would eventually give me the advantage. Adults loved Carolyn because she reminded them of Shirley Temple. Much later, reading Toni Morrison's *The Bluest Eye*, I learned what that icon had looked like from the other side of the racial divide. Like the blonde, blue-eyed dolls that Claudia, one of the protagonists, joyfully dismembers, Shirley stood for all the pretty little white girls who by some "magic" elicited gentle caresses from black women who offered their own daughters only harshness and neglect. To girls like Claudia, therefore, she was an object of both worship and intense hatred. The miracle of Diana Ross's triumph is that she was a little black girl who (in a way) got to be Shirley Temple. Meanwhile, back in 1965, there was Shirley Temple, on my porch, fighting to be Diana Ross. Ironic, isn't it?

And what can we *learn* from this odd, negative mirror-imaging?

One thing may be that envy knows no color, especially for women. I related to *The Bluest Eye*, although I was not black, because it so exactly described my own complicated feelings about my childhood friend. Partly, like Claudia, I saw my inferiority as racial, because

I was Jewish and Shirley/Carolyn was the epitome of shiksadom. But Morrison's novel also shows how images of ideal beauty oppress all real women, even the Shirleys themselves, no doubt, as they flatten themselves into pretty pictures on a screen.

Still, I don't think that in the matter of singing, all of us women are really in the same boat. One reason I had trouble giving my daughter a positive answer to her question is that even in 1965, when all the world seemed open to us, I didn't really believe that a white girl—even Carolyn—could sing as well as a black girl. And in my heart of hearts, right or wrong, I still think this way. Now I know this is racist and can't have any basis in biology, any more than the facial measurements the Nazis used to determine Jewishness. Nevertheless, it's hard to watch *Dreamgirls* without having this notion somehow reinforced. According to the movie, Deena (Diana), with a voice that is sweet rather than strong, light skin, and a model's figure, is pushed unjustly into becoming the leader of the group in the name of crossover. The record company executives correctly predict that white teens will find her easier to swallow than the original leader, big-voiced, big-bodied Effie (loosely modeled on Supreme Florence Ballard). The clear implication is that Deena's seeming less black than Effie is correlated with her singing less well. And apart from the movie, think about it. Doesn't Linda Ronstadt, covering Martha Reeves, sound, well, pale? Didn't we all laugh at Candice Bergen as Murphy Brown singing R-E-S-P-E-C-T? Wouldn't I trade places any day with Whitney Houston, maybe even now, just to have made a couple of those recordings?

Okay, I know these questions can be answered by yet another American cliché: We're all beautiful in our own way, or at least there may be more than one way to have a beautiful voice. *Dreamgirls* does let us see, eventually, that while Deena, as portrayed by Beyoncé, may not have the volume of Jennifer Hudson as Effie, she does have a lovely, subtle musical style of her own—just as Diana Ross proved she had when she portrayed the earlier crossover artist Billie Holiday in *Lady Sings the Blues*. Probably the rare gift of the golden larynx is bestowed on lucky individuals without regard to color or ethnicity, and maybe any of us, if we work hard, might turn out to sound, if not like Jennifer Hudson, maybe as good as Jennifer Hudson by some other criteria.

But somehow all of this may be beside the point. Because even if, theoretically, anyone could sing as well as Jennifer, or Beyoncé, or Diana, or Billie, there is still a question of entitlement. It takes a rich cultural tradition to make a real singer out of a lucky larynx. Naturally, we like to think the fruits of any culture are available to others to enjoy: one wouldn't want to argue that only a Norwegian should be allowed to perform Grieg. But as they used to say, you have to suffer if you want to sing the blues—a phrase I first heard, by the way, from the lips of David Bromberg, a "nice Jewish boy" who probably wishes he were Muddy Waters. And we have not all suffered equally. Another major theme of *Dreamgirls* is the appropriation of African-American talent by a white-dominated music industry: They liked it and they took it. On the other hand, we know what has happened, historically, to people of color who liked what white people had and tried to take it. Consider the stock character of the "tragic mulatta" in the 1927 musical *Showboat,* for example, or in the movie *Imitation of Life.* The girl (often played by a white actress) tries to "pass" and has to renounce her family, her past, her true self, and if she's ever found out, she loses everything. So, when a white girl thinks she'd give anything to sound like Aretha, she ought to stop and recall that this would mean selling her great-grandparents into slavery.

Cut from my porch in 1965 to the Pizza Hut in Hale'iwa, Hawaii, 2001, and you will see, in place of me and Carolyn, Violet and her best friend Emerald, age six, entertaining the patrons by singing and dancing along to Britney Spears' "Oops, I Did It Again" on the jukebox. Though the sight of the two little girls shaking their hips and singing, "I'm not that innocent" was a little creepy in a JonBenet Ramsay sort of way, it was also unbelievably cute. This was partly because of the sharp contrast in their appearance: fair Violet with her Shirley Temple curls, dark Emerald with her dozen little braids. We've come a long way, racially speaking, I suppose, when Emerald could feel just as entitled to be Britney as Violet did to be Raven. Of course, with Britney, we're not really talking about singing. But about those hip movements: how did they get from Africa and into the repertoire of this Shirley, or rather Lolita, of the 90's? And though she may cry, cry, cry in her lonely heart, did she really earn the right to dance like that?

I guess the only way we can even begin to pay what we owe for access to this cultural heritage is to acknowledge the debt and say thank you. And that's what I do in my heart every year, when the choir I belong to gets to perform for Black History Month, and this white girl is allowed to sing the blues.

Works Cited

Dreamgirls. DreamWorks and Paramount, 2006. Film.
Morrison, Toni. *The Bluest Eye.* NY: Vintage, 2007. Print.

Betty Sarvey Salek

Breathing

Breathing is supposed to be an involuntary action, like the beating of one's heart, designed to keep a body alive whether sleeping or speaking, walking or eating. But in the days following my husband's death, I often had to remind myself to breathe. I would lie in bed, conscious of the fact that it was not *our* bed, that it was the little bed upstairs, and then realize that I was not inhaling. It was as though I was waiting in limbo—for what I don't know. Perhaps I was waiting for a sign that he was all right, that we had done the right thing. Maybe I just wasn't used to breathing on my own. Once I discovered that my diaphragm wasn't doing its job, I would tell myself to inhale. And I would. And I would lie there, waiting, not knowing that I needed to exhale. But finally, I did exhale and the process would start all over again, and again. Finally, I would sleep. Morning would come randomly— 2:08 or 2:53…. Seldom did I sleep until dawn. Sometimes I would get up in the dark and write or make tea or just sit. Sometimes I would lie in bed and remind myself to breathe.

For three years I had been living a lie, pretending everything was normal, pretending he was not sick. How his friends did not notice his decline is still a mystery to me. But he insisted on keeping the cancer a secret, tucked into his lungs and his bones where it couldn't be seen. He met the disease with anger and defiance. I dealt with the disease and the anger and the defiance by creating a room in my head where I could toss it all in and lock the door: a Victorian "box room" that I could visit or not as needed. I never deluded myself. But I didn't need to live it every second of every day. I couldn't change the outcome; therefore, I didn't dwell on it. I knew from the day the doctor delivered the death sentence that my husband would not receive a reprieve. No last-minute call from the governor commuting this to life in prison. Three years in this prison was enough. Two months with the car keys hidden was too much. I hid the keys to the gun cabinet, as well, after I caught him standing in front of it, contemplating. Surely, he told me, God would not condemn him for putting an end to the pain. I told him to go into the woods, then, and die a natural death under a tree and the autumn sky. He chose to die in his own bed, though, telling me he didn't care if it was selfish. When he apologized for putting me through all this, I thought, "Of all the things you have put me through in the last thirty-something years, this is the one thing you do not need to apologize for."

On the day my husband died, our daughter was scheduled for a sonogram. We were to discover the sex of her baby. Our first grandchild. I was supposed to accompany her and her husband. She had hoped her father would be well enough to come, but the effort of staying alive long enough to hold that baby brought him more anguish than he, or I, could endure. Days before, I had arranged for our church deacon to watch over him while I went to the appointment. I knew he would be well cared for. But how could I leave, after the Hospice nurse told me he had short hours to live? How could I leave when my husband was dying? How could I leave, knowing he would be gone when I returned?

Every two hours throughout the night and into that day I had 'administered' morphine, his response to fight me surging up from his oblivion. The physical act, though, was easier than the emotional duress. I couldn't shake the feeling that I was putting the cat down. I had to remind myself that this had been his decision: that I had asked him after a day of less pain if he understood what we were doing and did he want to reconsider. Yes, he understood. No, he wouldn't change his mind. This was what he wanted. All day I had lain with him, holding his hand, talking, not talking, telling him it was okay to go. He waited for his first son to arrive, summoned from out of town to say goodbye. He waited for his daughter to come and go. He waited for me to leave. Yes, I went to that sonogram. He waited for the second son, also summoned from far away. He waited until he was ready.

For so long I had lived the lie. For so long I had pretended that nothing was wrong. I knew I had done all I could for him. I had to do for the living, now. I went to that sonogram. At 3:36 we saw little limbs flailing and the tiny 'stem' of a boy. We cried. We cried because they had wanted a boy. We cried because we had wanted Daddy to be there. And then we went to buy baby boy balloons. We went to Macy's to pay my charge card bill—it was due that day and who knew when it would be paid if not now. For so long our little secret had been locked in my box room, I didn't need to *pretend* this day was not like any other. For me, it *wasn't* any different. I almost stopped in the shoe department, a surreal euphoria overtaking my mission. Instead, with a brief niggling of guilt, I glided to customer service, wrote my check, and reluctantly returned to the car. "I want to go home, but I don't want to go home," my daughter and I both admitted.

I knew before I opened the door. My husband had slipped away sometime between then and now. Yes, the deacon said. Just after our second son had said his peace, while he sat alone with his father—the deacon and the Hospice nurse and his brother waiting in the next room. Yes, the deacon said. At 3:30. It was just enough time. He had wanted to know if his daughter carried a girl or a boy, but he couldn't wait for the balloons.

He had died in his bed as he had wanted. And now I sleep in the little bed upstairs. The grandson he never saw ensures that I breathe without thinking.

Amy M. Schiffman

L & M

For the first thirty-seven years, my parents didn't know the deli had a name. From the time they bought the brownstone on Fifteenth Street, my mother referred to the grocery store around the corner on Seventh Avenue, along with the people who ran it, as "The Maltese." It was not a derogatory term. The proprietors of the shop were the only people she had ever met who came from the island of Malta. It was more like reverse racial profiling, a way to differentiate them from the other deli owners in the neighborhood: They weren't Korean, nor were they Dominican—the ethnic groups that predominated behind the deli counters in their Chelsea neighborhood.

Close to four decades after moving into the brownstone and fifteen years into the new millennium, during which time their once-dreary neighborhood had evolved into a cleaner quarter, a magnet for the newly wealthy, my mother, Ruth, turned 90 and my father, Irving, turned 91. They were the oldest couple in a neighborhood populated with younger—and richer—folks. Going to the Maltese to get *The New York Times* had

181

long been Irving's morning ritual. But last winter he aged noticeably. He lacked energy in the morning, so on a clear, early December day, it was Ruth who hobbled out, with the aid of her cane, to buy the paper. That's when she noticed the letters L&M stenciled on the green awning over the door to the grocery store. Had the name always been there? Or had they recently added the lettering to compete with the newer, jauntily colored awnings in Chelsea and the nearby and even more upscale West Village?

My parents didn't frequent the restaurants and cafes with the red or navy-blue awnings whose offerings apparently came from "farm to table." They preferred the few remaining older establishments where they could have a dish of pasta, and a glass of wine, for a reasonable price, as Irving put it, "without a lecture from the waiter about where the porcini mushrooms came from." Ruth and Irving are foodies of an earlier era. When they were younger, they traveled and learned to cook the foods they enjoyed in Italy and France when they came home to Manhattan. They weren't "food bores," as one of their friends typified the younger generation of food fanatics, but they were particular, so they went out of their way to get the meals they preferred, and rarely bought prepared food from behind the counter at L&M.

"The Maltese" served buttered bagels in the morning and hero sandwiches at lunch. It was the kind of convenient deli/grocery that was now disappearing from the streets of Manhattan: just necessities—no gluten-free options, no cappuccinos or lattes. Because L&M was so close to my parents' front door, Irving often stopped by for something he'd forgotten at the supermarket: a quart of milk, an extra can of tuna. The proprietors knew him and my mother well, just as they knew many of the

182

customers' names, and anticipated their coffee orders: black, or light and sweet, and which paper—*Post, News* or *Times*—they were going to choose from the rack at the front of the store.

In January, my father's fatigue became worse. He was diagnosed with congestive heart failure, and when the weather got bad, he caught a cold which turned into pneumonia. He spent a few nights in NYU Hospital, after which time, to my mother's enormous relief, he was sent home. But even though he was judged well enough to be home, he just couldn't seem to recover his strength, despite visits to myriad doctors. My mother was having trouble taking care of an elderly invalid. After all, she was herself ninety. Not least of her problems was how to keep them both fed. Irving had long ago taken over the cooking and much of the shopping. Now that Ruth walked with a cane, cooking was a challenge. She needed more help, in general, but was loath to admit it. Neighbors like Stephie, owner of a brownstone across the street, were extremely helpful, but once the snow turned to ice on the sidewalk, even her visits became infrequent.

One particularly frigid January day, the doorbell rang around noon. Ruth found her cane and hobbled to answer. Outside the entryway, wrapped in a grey parka, was one of the stock boys who worked in the back of L&M. He said that his boss Larry (the L of L & M) had noticed that Irving hadn't been in lately. Larry wondered if they needed anything. Ruth admitted that with Irving sick, she had fallen behind in her grocery shopping, hadn't even thought about what to make for lunch that day. All they had in the house was canned soup. The young man left and returned in 20 minutes bearing a brown bag containing grilled cheese sandwiches and meatball heroes, two of L & M's specialties. My mother

183

set the table, unwrapped the sandwiches, ushered Irving over. Once seated, she gobbled her grilled cheese gratefully while urging a reluctant Irving to eat a meatball sandwich. He finished half. The other half she wrapped in deli paper and put it in the refrigerator.

In April, both of my parents were feeling stronger. One afternoon, Ruth asked the housekeeper Cassie (my sister's one-time nanny, who now came to help my parents once a week) to put a chair out in front of the building so that she could sit in the sun, and see what was going on in the neighborhood. Stephie, stepping out of her similar blue-painted brownstone on the south side of the street, saw her sitting outside and came across to visit and gossip.

"Did you hear about L&M?" Stephie asked.

"No, what about The Maltese?" asked my mother.

"They are leaving when their lease is up. The landlord raised the rent."

The two women shook their heads ruefully. They had been landlords on this block for almost 40 years. They were friendly with the younger woman who had recently acquired the apartment building next door to my parents' in a divorce settlement. Her building housed the adjacent grocery, making her L&M's landlord. She was a newer generation of property owner, whose values apparently did not line up with those of the older residents of the neighborhood. She might have well been one of those marauding yuppies who were ruining things in Chelsea. She was driving out The Maltese.

Irving shouted from inside the dark apartment,

"Ruth, have you seen my glasses?"

"As if I would move his glasses," she mumbled to Stephie, then shouted back, "No I haven't seen them, but try the bathroom sink. You always leave them there. Did

184

you hear what Stephie said about The Maltese?" Irving's hearing was pretty bad; he couldn't possibly have heard. "The landlord is raising the rent and they're leaving."

"I cannot hear you," responded Irving.

"Some yuppie place will come in there," Ruth said to Stephie. "We'll have to go all the way to Eighth Avenue to get our paper!"

"Where are my glasses?" Irving shouted again.

Ruth waved goodbye to Stephie, and hobbled into the house to help Irving look for his glasses. At her age, there wasn't much point in worrying about the future of the local grocery store. Still, the Maltese had turned out to be great neighbors. It would be sad to lose them. And she would never forget that hot grilled cheese sandwich on that frigid January day. When there was snow on the ground, and the temperature was below zero, those surprise sandwiches from L&M had been lifesavers.

Jan Sidebotham

Speech at First Coed
Hamilton Graduation
May 27, 1979

In the spring of 1979, Hamilton College celebrated its first coed graduation. Kirkland College, its coordinate institution, had ceased to exist the previous year when the two schools merged under somewhat acrimonious circumstances. It was a tumultuous time as two distinct colleges with divergent philosophies set out to graduate two student bodies as one.

I was told that my speech today should be a mixture of sentiment and humor and that I should make people feel good. I sense behind that advice a fear that I will mar this ceremony with stridency and divisiveness. Why might I create bitterness? Because I lost my college. I am a former Kirkland student receiving a degree from

Hamilton. Like some other women students at Hamilton, I am not entirely happy with Kirkland's fate and not entirely convinced that the merger has gone through smoothly, as many insist it has. Most of all, I'm afraid that within a few years, even without malevolence, Hamilton will manage to wipe out all traces of Kirkland.

For those of you who don't know, Kirkland was the school across the street in which all the women in the class were originally enrolled and which has since folded and been absorbed by Hamilton in a move loosely and inaccurately called a merger. What we lost in losing Kirkland was an alternative, and in that alone, we lost much. Each of us as individuals can seek out his or her own alternate routes to learning, but it is a rare opportunity to be backed up by an institution in that search. Our class was lucky enough to enjoy that opportunity for three years.

At Kirkland, there was the sense that students were trusted. Whether manifested in the first-name basis that is between most students and faculty or in policies such as independent study programs that depended on a student's self-motivation, there was evidence that the administration assumed that students were grown-ups. The fact that one could design her own major indicated that the school had a respect for the student's individuality. The use of evaluations as opposed to grades also contributed to the student's sense of her own uniqueness and was based on the belief that students were interested in learning for its own sake, not for the sake of getting on the Dean's List. Evaluations also encouraged students to compete with themselves rather than with others. In many ways, Kirkland's policies testified to the administration's and faculty's confidence in students. Kirkland had her problems, but one of her fine points was the dignity which she assigned to students.

In conversations about this speech, various people have urged me not to be divisive. That exhortation for unity, at any cost, has become some kind of watchword for the post-merger era. Unity, peace, congeniality have all become ultimate goals. They may be worthy goals, but they may also be attained at exorbitant cost, in which case we should examine our values.

Is unity possible, or even desirable, in an academic community? After all, what's so wrong with division? Why are we so afraid of it? Certainly, we cannot expect people to agree with each other; can we expect them to sacrifice convictions only for the sake of harmony? Unity is important, but it should not be the final criterion, especially in an educational institution. Supposedly, education is all about learning and discovering. How can we learn and discover without challenging, questioning, and criticizing? When we ask for unity, at any cost, we come dangerously close to imperialism. What ends up happening is that the minority is required to agree with the majority's decisions, regardless of how firmly the minority believes in its own judgments. When one party says to another, "Please don't be divisive," it can mean, "Your opinion doesn't count; mine does." Rebelliousness for its own sake is destructive, and we cannot encourage people to be demagogues. But we don't have to fear dissent. If you can't make waves in the academy, where can you make them?

Don't we expect a certain amount of division in a place where opinions are being asserted? If my graduation speech turns out to be divisive, it's not that I've created division among you. The fact is that I am speaking to a divided audience. To think that a speaker

188

could take any position without disagreeing with a part of the audience is naïve at best. Sure, everyone wants to get along, and peace and harmony are noble goals, but what is the quality of the peace if there are people keeping their challenges and criticisms to themselves? Is it harmony when one person is free to state his or her opinion and a companion, for the sake of unity, is urged to nod in agreement whether or not, in fact, he or she does agree? That seems like a cheap peace to me.

People can have different views and still cooperate. I think that's the ideal educational setting— where peace is highly valued, but not to the point of requiring us to sacrifice truth.

One thing that strikes me as sad about our country is that, in an effort to be an American, many of us have lost our individual heritages. We have hidden, to the point of losing, our cultural differences. The great melting pot has indeed melted French, African, German, Latin American, Chinese, etc. into a bunch of Americans whose cultural heritage may only be represented by McDonald's golden arches.

In the same way, Hamilton's quest for unity may lead only to attaining homogeneity, and in the loss of our differences, we'll lose our individuality—eventually, we'll lose ourselves.

You can come to work out and even cherish differences. When I first came here, I hated the modern architecture at Kirkland and was much more drawn to the older buildings at Hamilton. During the last four years, I have come to appreciate the new structures across the street while maintaining my fondness for Carnegie and the Chapel. We can see the value in different kinds of architecture: why can't we likewise see the value in different kinds of attitudes and ideas? Just as the modern

Burke Library has been integrated into the Stryker campus, why can't different educational approaches be accepted within Hamilton's structure?

The school could capitalize on what former Kirkland students and faculty have to offer and could start making distinctions based on what's good and bad, rather than on what's "Kirkland" and what's "Hamilton." The Kirkland-Hamilton battle is history now. It's time to judge ideas for what they are, not as party platforms for either faction. The acceptance or rejection of any proposal—whether it affects academic or social life—should depend on the intrinsic value of such a proposal, not on whether it reminds us of Hamilton or Kirkland. For example, if it is a good idea to have faculty residents live in dorms, then let us adopt the idea because it is a good one, not because it smacks of one college or the other. No academic policy should be judged as if it were a symbol for an institution.

The Kirkland class of '79 has gotten the education of a lifetime. We have lived through the folding of our college. How many times does one live through a transformation like that?—the shift from one era to another? We're a remnant of the old Kirkland cloth. At times we've clashed badly with Hamilton's colors. At other times we've matched well. And whether we deny it or not, we are woven into the new Hamilton fabric. We are children of two eras—or perhaps children of neither era.

Both Kirkland and Hamilton have left their mark on this graduating class. I hope that will be the case for every graduating class that follows.

A house divided cannot stand. Hamilton will find its unity somehow. It can achieve unity either by waiting for three years to pass and more or less expunging the memory of Kirkland, or it can make a genuine and creative effort to preserve the best of both colleges. If Hamilton doesn't choose soon to hold onto Kirkland's gifts, we will surely lose them.

The most intelligent way to deal with division is neither to ignore it nor to foster it but to confront it and work out whatever problem it creates. That final stage, after differences have been recognized and dealt with, is real unity, real peace.

Judy Silverstein Gray

The Good War

For Kendrick Folsom, being drafted into World War II catapulted him into an adventure and the horrors of war, simultaneously.

Known as "the good war," it was waged to preserve democracy. But the reality on the front lines involved the loss of friends, bloody injuries, and a constant pounding from the German artillery forces. The stories shared by Folsom bear that out.

"We made personal and significant contributions, and the reality is—it was hard-won," says Folsom, 77. "We lost many young men and had many sad moments."

A native of Six Mile Creek in eastern Hillsborough County (near Tampa, Florida), he found being drafted offered a chance to see the world. Local enlistees were provided a meal, courtesy of the Army, at the Columbia Restaurant in Ybor City.

"We called it the Last Supper," Folsom quips.

Married at 17, Folsom and his wife, Pauline, were expecting their first child when the Army called him up in 1943. He recalls induction at Camp Blanding, in Starke.

"We ate, slept, and walked in a raincoat and Army boots, and that's it, not even underwear," he says. "And I didn't like it one bit—it was hot, and there were 200 to 300 of us. We were just like convicts."

At Fort McClellan, Alabama, Folsom received infantry training. He was schooled as a radioman, in communications. To pass the downtime, he brought along his coveted electric guitar, a spiffy $35 Silvertone bought from the Sears, Roebuck and Co. catalog.

"I played every night and met other fellas who were also musicians," he says.

He continues to play every Thursday night at the Bluegrass Parlor on Busch Boulevard. Married for 58 years, he's the father of three, grandfather of eight, and great-grandfather of three.

In Basic Training, Folsom says, he was a strapping man who enjoyed the grueling 16 weeks at Fort McClellan.

"I was young and intrigued by the obstacle course. And I was meeting people from all over the place."

His company shipped out early, not taking advantage of the furlough President Roosevelt had promised all GIs. Classified as a rifleman—and making $45 a month—Folsom sailed on one of the first convoys overseas. Initially, he thought he might be headed to the South Pacific, but the ship arrived in North Africa after 13 days at sea.

"But I had no fear, I was young and indestructible," Folsom says.

Africa's climate was perplexing. It was 110 degrees in the shade by day and freezing at night. The infantry slept on hay, eating K-rations and C-rations.

"Every meal of every day was the same—cheese in the morning, SPAM at noon," he says.

Folsom and fellow GIs encountered only light fighting while stationed in Africa, where camaraderie was strong among the troops.

"If you ran into someone from Florida, you had an instant friend," the Tampa native says. "I actually met some boys from Ybor City—straight off."

His trusted guitar and the occasional movie offered by the Army provided some distraction from war. Folsom recalls the makeshift military theater: helmets for seats and a bedsheet stretched across two poles for the screen. As the Germans retreated from Africa, Folsom and his unit got new orders and shipped off to Italy.

Destination: Salerno

"We figured Italy would be a cakewalk," he says.

But the Germans, known for their sophisticated intelligence system, were always one step ahead of American troops. When Folsom and his fellow GIs landed on the beaches of Salerno on Sept. 9, 1943, they were ambushed.

The battle of Salerno was the first invasion of Europe and a treacherous battle for the Americans. Positioned up in the hills, the Germans fired down on the Americans, with terrain offering little cover. As troops landed on the beaches, heavy artillery fire punctuated the day.

"My lands, there were casualties," Folsom remembers, shaking his head and recalling the chaos.

"As we lugged our 50-pound packs up the beach, looking for shrubbery and a place to hide, my hands were numb and we were frightened, but we had something to fight for."

Folsom offers stirring accounts of young troops working their way up the beachhead. With smoke and fire everywhere, he became separated from his battalion. Later, they fought their way north, losing men along the way.

Those memories of war are still tough for Folsom, his eyes welling up in remembrance of his buddies.

"But we were young and invincible, and that's the beauty of youth," he says. "There were hours where we sat very still in waist-deep water that was freezing cold. We'd whisper to one another and move very, very slowly, advancing mostly at night."

North of Salerno, the battalion fought its way through San Pietro, where more than half of Folsom's battalion was lost. That battle drew the attention of famed war correspondent Ernie Pyle, who interviewed Folsom—and others—about their experiences.

Fast-forward to January 1944. American troops continued to slug it out with the Germans in Italy. In places like the Abbey Casino and the Rapido River, Folsom and his fellow soldiers encountered horrific fighting. Near the river, Folsom timed the 60-second breaks in artillery fire with his GI-issued watch, affording himself and four buddies the chance to run for it. They ducked into craters before the next three-minute barrage rained down. Despite heavy rain and cold temperatures, the five made it back to their lines. Folsom's new Yankee friend from New Hampshire, Everett Grant, dubbed him the *Rapido Kid* for calculating a way to escape the heavy fire.

Folsom's division also helped fight to protect the beachhead at Enzio. It rained for weeks as the troops were pinned by German soldiers stationed in the mountains. The phrase "Enzio Beachhead Express" referred to the two largest guns the Germans owned.

"They could only fire once a day because the barrel needed 24 hours to cool down," Folsom says.

As they pushed on to Rome in May, American troops finally captured one of the guns. During one point in the bloody battle, German soldiers pinned Folsom and his friends into foxholes. Pulling the canvas roof over the top, they crouched down as tanks rode overhead. When they crept out, Folsom discovered his trusty guitar had been crushed.

As his battalion made it to Rome, sniper fire was visible, although local citizens celebrated when the troops arrived, serving brandy and wine. As the 141st Infantry piled into the city, they learned of the impending invasion in Normandy. But as Rome fell on June 5, troops heard high waters delayed the invasion in France. On the outskirts of the city, fighting still erupted. On June 11, a shell hit the barn where Folsom and other soldiers were hiding.

The explosion injured his right side, arm, hand, and left leg. Lying motionless under the hay, Folsom held his breath as German soldiers walked through, poking their pitchforks within inches of where he laid still. Later that day, his American rescuers arrived. They draped him over the hood of a Jeep and drove 30 miles on rocky roads to a field first-aid station. One of four brothers fighting overseas during the war, Folsom says survival was a family matter.

"I had to get through it. I'd promised my mother I'd come home."

He was shipped to a hospital in West Virginia for a final surgery, and then to Miami to convalesce. When a physician asked him how many days a man should spend in combat, Folsom said, "One day in combat is one day too many."

He's never changed his mind.

"Being in combat changes the way you look at the world," says Folsom, adding that it was a full five years before he could attend a funeral.

"I lost so many friends over there."

Folsom's 36th division received a presidential unit citation from Franklin D. Roosevelt for its participation in the battle at Salerno. For injuries sustained while in Rome, he received a Purple Heart with an oak leaf cluster, and a Bronze Star for valor. He is most proud, however, of his combat infantry badge, recognizing distinguished battle service.

While Folsom is fiercely proud of how American troops performed in World War II, he is most touched by the camaraderie he felt and the friendships he made. He corresponded with Grant and the two visited every other year starting in 1984. Though his longtime friend recently died, he remains proud to tell his war stories. Yet he's most comfortable talking to fellow veterans who understand the complexities—and the tragedies of battle.

Folsom also enjoys recalling his youth. He remembers seeing his first automobile, first airplane, first talking movie, and his first blimp.

"There will never be another generation like us because we saw everything firsthand," he says. "I wouldn't take anything in the world for the experiences I had in combat.... It was an important war that had to be fought. Without those battles," he says, "the world would have been very different."

He leans in to deliver a message.

"You know, I'd do it again to keep the world safe, but war is something no one really wants to go through."

Caroline BD Smith

Natalie Babbitt: Writing Serious Fantasy

"I love words—I'm a word person. Writing is hard work. It's hard work for everyone—especially if you're a housewife and a mother—but I'm one of those people who want to have the whole package."

Natalie Babbitt, wife of Kirkland's President Samuel F. Babbitt, has written and illustrated eight children's books, the most recent of which, entitled *Tuck Everlasting*, was selected by *The New York Times* as "one of the best books of the year for children."

Originally Natalie and Sam Babbitt wanted to be collaborators on children's book writing and illustrating; in fact, the first book Natalie illustrated, *The 49th Magician*, was written by Sam, although Natalie claims credit for the title. "Sam started out wanting to be a novelist," she said.

Now Natalie is the writer in the family, and she limits her prose to children's books. "I have no desire to write adult fiction as it is these days," she said. "There is a lot of self-exposure that goes on in that."

The 'Everyman' Questions

"I write about things that interest me. These are not the kind of things that have conclusions; they're usually just speculative. I'm more interested in general ideas—the 'life questions', the 'Everyman' type of thing. This has gone out of style now, but it will come back someday," she said.

"I'm interested in being able to use fantasy in certain kinds of ways to express ideas. Some ideas are always around; these interest me—not drugs and unwed mothers," said Natalie, explaining why adult fiction writing does not appeal to her. "These ideas won't survive."

"I'm not interested in surviving as a writer—it's just that the ideas that are interesting are the ones that will survive," she said.

Most writers find it difficult to enter and to stay in the children's book field because "children's books have no status in the adult world," said Natalie. Children's authors are told to "go into serious writing," and this has kept a lot of people out of the field. "Children's writing is supposed to be a trivial thing to do," she said.

Not Little Adults

Natalie thinks that the reason children's books have little status in the adult world has to do with the "national attitude toward children." Rather than treating childhood as one of the most important times of life, people "try to form children into little adults." They do not accept the idea that "children's metaphors are just as

199

important to them at that time of life as ours are to us," Natalie said.

"I'm not a great child-lover," Natalie admitted. "I wouldn't want to be a kindergarten teacher, but children are what we all once were, and what we are not comes out of that."

"Anyone who goes into children's writing without being interested in their own childhood is not being honest about it," she said.

"I remember my own fears, dreams...once doors are open, stuff comes flooding back. It's one of the best ways I know to gain respect for a stage of our lives that has been greatly downgraded."

"A Taste for Blood"

"It has taken the world a long time to realize that children are 3-D human beings, that they have feelings for violence—a taste for blood—just like adults do. Society has taken the view that violence is a corruptive influence. There are a lot of things that children share with adults—especially fear, hates of various kinds, and love too," she said.

"Children are not all alike—they are just as individualistic as adults are. Children have been an under-graded, patronized group," said Natalie.

Tuck Everlasting, which came out exactly one year ago, is "based on an idea I've always been interested in—thinking of time as a circle," she said. Her family were pioneers, said Natalie. "My mother felt very close to the land, and you can't be involved without having a strong sense of the pattern," she said.

Tuck Everlasting

The setting for *Tuck Everlasting* is an actual place—a town called Forestport, where the Babbitts have a home, in the foothills of the Adirondacks. The cover drawing is taken directly from a photograph taken by Sam Babbitt, showing the lake, woods, and their cabin. "It is very isolated, and you can't escape feeling a part of the changing of nature," she said.

"A lot of children's books deliberately avoid discussing death," Natalie said. "But it's important to talk about it as an entire cycle rather than an end," Natalie said. "*Charlotte's Web,* by E. B. White, is beautiful in that respect."

"The image of the Ferris wheel in the prologue of *Tuck Everlasting* comes from summers spent in a small town in central Ohio," said Natalie, "when in the amusement park the sound of the roller coaster was ever-present. All rides are circles, and the Ferris wheel emerged as a symbol—one thing that went around," she said.

Natalie grew up in Ohio and attended Smith College, where she majored in studio art.

She "didn't learn anything useful," she said. "Studio art was not an academic discipline," and she had "no way to teach it." She married Sam Babbitt two weeks after she graduated from college and had three children before beginning to write.

Her Boys an Impatient Audience

Her children were not the best audience for her books, she said. The boys soon "lost patience with being read aloud to," but after her editor proclaimed a work to be good, she read it to them, and "if they didn't like it, it didn't matter," she said. "The idea of having to have children to write for children is nonsense."

Seven years ago, Natalie taught a writing course at Kirkland, and a course in illustrating the following year. She said she thought these were not successful because they were only "good for those students who were already seriously interested." She said she is "not a teacher, but a professional" and did not have the academic point of view.

She has kept in touch with several of her students, and one, Steve Krensky, who graduated in the Hamilton class of '75, has sold his second children's novel and will be teaching a Winter Study course in Children's Writing at Kirkland this January.

"Teaching is hard—exhausting—and it does take a lot of psychic energy away from writing, but I get involved," she said. The main problem is that "there isn't continuous, uninterrupted time to work."

Entranced with Students

"Next year I will try to cut myself out from everything else—but I get entranced with students." She now works with several students on senior projects as "a kind of specialty." "I can concentrate on bringing about individual personal growth, and talk about individual writing problems, which is very hard to do in class."

Six or seven times a year, Natalie Babbitt writes reviews for *The New York Times* magazine, but all of her business is done over the phone. "I haven't been to New York in a couple of years," she said. When her manuscripts reach the stage for editing, she's often "on the phone for three hours at a stretch."

She describes her editor as a "fussy, pedantic young man. We argue about commas, single words...we have a glorious time," she said. "I've never worked with anyone but him."

Thumping Podiums

Another thing that has been taking up Natalie's time is "thumping podiums." On the day after Thanksgiving, she will be going to Chicago to address the National Council of Teachers of English. She doesn't like to travel, but "I like to get up there to thump and rant," she said.

"What they expect me to talk about is the 'creative impulse'—what funny thing happened on the way to the typewriter," she said. "They want to be amused, but I feel that there are a lot of important things that need to be talked about."

"The world of children's books is a hotbed; there is a fascinating turmoil going on," Natalie said. "I get worried about the quality of most of the things that come out—a lot of it is awful." A common feeling about children's books is that they don't necessarily have to be well written," she said. "Anything you don't think has to be done well is easy."

Two thousand children's books are now published annually, but we could go 50 years without having more written, she said. "Children don't change that much," she said.

The Standards Then

Some of the authors she enjoyed as a child were Lewis Carroll, Rudyard Kipling, and Booth Tarkington. These were "people who loved the language and used it as a tool to play with and manipulate," she said. The worlds of Charles Kingsley, Hawthorne, Twain, and A. A.

Milne were "the standards (of books) that we grew up with," she said.

Children don't read as much today as they used to, and although television has taken the blame for children not reading, Natalie said she does not think it is all the fault of TV. "The pace of the world has picked up," she said.

"Reading is a way of absorbing things gradually, a kind of contemplative thing to do, and impatience has a lot to do with children not reading. Communication today is a lot more visual," Natalie said.

Children's books are not as popular with college students as they were five years ago," Natalie said. For a while, there was a lot of reading of children's literature— "I think it was a manifestation of looking for simplified answers," she said.

Natalie Babbitt is presently working on a story that takes a man through his life from birth to death; it may work out to be three books, or one book in three parts, she said. "So far I've done about 50 pages, and he's only eight years old."

"Nobody has been able to successfully define the cutoff point from the child into the adult; there isn't one," she said. "Childhood is a stage of life without edges. All of us retain a large chunk from one stage to the next. It's all a great blur."

Constance Stellas

Astrology: A Window Into My Profession

I didn't plan to be an astrologer, but it has been my profession for the past twenty-five years. Many people say they don't believe in such nonsense. That's fine with me. They might be right, but I see people checking their horoscope in the newspaper even after they tell me they think it is silly. We all want to believe that the stars are on our side. Feeling connected to the cosmos can give comfort and support in a fast-changing and scary world. Whether you believe or not, Astrology works, and for me, it has been an incredibly interesting way to gain self-knowledge, look at the world, and help clients.

An astrology chart is basically a map of where the Sun, Moon, and planets were located in the heavens at the time of birth. Twins are sometimes an astrological conundrum as they can be born one minute apart and have virtually the same chart but oftentimes very different lives. I am glad the Octomom never called me. I think I would freak out looking at those charts. But for the most part, each person's chart is an individual blueprint of all the energies that create a unique person. The chart reveals a person's essence: body, mind, and spirit.

Computers have made my life a lot easier because a computer program can calculate a chart in five seconds. I hand calculated charts for a number of years and was fast, but still, it took at least twenty minutes. Software also can interpret a chart. I don't like this trend in astrology because although interpretations can give some knowledge, the program gives the same interpretation for anyone born at that time, date, and year. Human beings are more nuanced, and what I like best is the dialogue between the stars, myself, and a client.

A person's chart reveals basic talents, temperament, challenges, and the themes of a person's life—this life and past lives. Astrology is part of many religions where reincarnation is assumed. Some Westerners find this difficult, but I think considering past lives is an efficient system that outlines the soul's evolution and growth throughout eons. I don't spend a lot of time discussing past lives with clients because many people cherish the notion they were kings or queens or other notables. I have had a lot of Joan of Arc past lifers. It is rarely the case that a person was one of the great historical figures...and besides, there are no soul DNA tests to confirm it. Best to concentrate on this lifetime. Knowing about a past life's energy can help a person understand certain habits and tendencies this time around. In some cases, particularly with addiction problems, a past life understanding can be very therapeutic.

Some of the most interesting experiences in my astrology practice occurred while I worked on Sirius XM radio. Once a week I was on the show Broadminded. I was the Astrology Broad and took calls from people all over the country. Many of the callers were lady truckers. They all had satellite radio in the truck, and, as they barreled down the road, they called in and asked about health, boyfriends, family, money, career, etc. It always worried me when the chart showed a potentially tense outcome to a question. I was afraid I would hear an 18-wheeler going off the highway. I usually asked people to pull over while we chatted about the chart and, as far as I know, I didn't lose anybody while I was on the radio.

I spend a lot of time speaking and thinking about time, that is, how a particular time period influences a person's life at the moment and will in the future. The movement of the planets is fixed and regular, and we can locate where any planet will be next year or in fifty years. As the planets move, they make different patterns that affect the birth chart. Planetary patterns and movement influence individuals as well as leaders, nations, and businesses. Every country has a chart for the day and time they were "born." In the current election year, astrologers are very busy comparing the candidates' birth charts with the chart for the United States. The candidate whose chart connects most closely with the USA chart will win.

Besides specific predictions for individuals, the patterns in the sky give us an understanding of the tenor of the times. This part of astrology is called *mundane astrology* and is very good for forecasting world events, economic downturns, boom cycles, and war. For example, we are in a time period right now where reality structures and governments (signified by Saturn) are beginning a major thrust of transformation that will last until 2022. This transformation will be in governments, the global economic situation, and climate change.

Could knowing this pattern prevent difficulties? Unfortunately, probably not because many horrifying events are ruled by Uranus, the planet that represents unpredictable chaos. The best way to use astrological information or predictions about the world is to take extra precautions when there are acutely inharmonious patterns. This is basically what Joan Quigley did for Ronald Reagan. Quigley did not initiate policy but found the best times to ensure the outcomes that Reagan wanted. And she kept him safe. Nancy consulted Joan after Reagan had been shot. No ancient person would be surprised that astrology is useful to leaders. In ancient Rome, it was a capital offense to calculate and study the emperor's chart because a seer could take advantage of power shifts. I would not want the job of advising a president, but I am sure following astrology would improve outcomes for governments and nations. It is interesting to me how often events occur that are described by the planetary patterns.

Some of the most frequent questions that I can answer regard the auspicious times for various events. Some people call about good days for important meetings, medical procedures, and travel. There are definitely good days and not-so-good days for any activity. Choosing a good day does not necessarily mean that everything will be perfect but that you can maximize your chances of a positive outcome. Regarding travel, especially flying, I have tracked air crashes for years, and in every case, there were one or two astrological markers for difficulties. Thankfully, most flights are safe, but when there are more than three tension aspects in a chart, I advise the client to choose another day and time to fly.

Questions about safety and health outcomes for surgery raise the inevitable baseline question: Will I live? Or, more pointedly, when will I die? There is a long tradition in astrology not to reveal the answer to this question. If an astrologer poses the question for himself or herself, the chart will not yield an answer. In addition to ethical considerations, the astrological patterns can indicate many crises in a person's life where it could be possible for a person to pass into spirit. Any good astrologer can see these critical periods. In these situations, I discuss the time period for the crisis but not the outcome. The truth is that a person has some control over the time he or she passes on, and this is perhaps the most individual decision in life. An astrologer also should not answer the question of when a relative will die. Sometimes people's motivations are not all that high-minded. I have had people ask me when their tiresome aunt would kick the bucket because they stood to inherit a lot of money. Forecasting or even calculating a chart for this reason is a misuse of the "divine science."

I like looking at the big cosmic picture. Watching my own chart and my family's is a perspective that comforts me even when the news is not to my liking. In terms of world events, I feel outraged, amazed, and sometimes surprised by how events correspond to the rhythm of the planets. Ancient sailors navigated by the stars. Today we have very sophisticated instruments to locate ourselves anywhere in the world, and yet we still wonder. Astrology is a platform for this wonder.

Janet Sternberg

Unstable Users:
Displacement and Distraction
as Perils of the Transition
to Digital Media

Transitions to new technologies don't always have predictable or favorable consequences. We recognize the promise of digital media, but we must also raise questions about the possible peril of this transition. Digital media give rise to certain problems of stability, including displacement and distraction.

Displacement in space and time results from new forms of presence. We combine new forms of virtual presence with traditional forms of physical presence, creating mixed environments where we're partially present in several places at once yet not fully present anywhere at all. Increasingly, concepts like "here" and "now" confuse us, and we're unsure of where and with whom we are at any given moment.

Distraction is promoted by new forms of attention. We do many things simultaneously, multi-tasking and dividing our attention among a broad repertoire of communication techniques and technologies, both traditional and digital. We rarely do one thing at a time sequentially, single-tasking. But human attention is finite, and combining direct sensory perception with indirect technologically-mediated perception, we often lose focus and concentration and the sense of knowing and controlling what we're doing.

Introduced by digital media, new forms of presence and attention change our relationships with ourselves, with others, and with our environments, bringing unexpected consequences such as problems of displacement and distraction. By trying to understand negative as well as positive effects, what technologies undo as well as what they do, we stand a better chance of stabilizing our technological environments, and decreasing the peril and increasing the promise of digital media.

Isabel Weinger Nielsen

Changing Focus

Every time I walked into the darkroom the sensations were the same: the smell of the fixer both irritating and welcoming, the black satin curtain rubbing smoothly against my cheek as I entered, the comforting blackness inside the room. There was no sound. I clicked on the enlarger, momentarily. Clicked off. The paper floated on chemicals, then sank.

Quiet. Surrounding me, enclosing me. The silence excited me. When I turned the paper over the silence became a vision, a shape, a photograph. Shades of grays and blacks, becoming their own unique design. Thirty seconds, a line. Forty seconds, an eye. Fifty-five seconds, some hair. And finally, a face, my own face staring up at me. I wanted to shout as the image came into focus. I could feel myself churning and bubbling inside.

That was then. It's now forty years later, the 21st century, the digital age. As if by magic I can take photographs with my phone, I can use a camera without film to record special events. Everyone is doing it. Where do I fit in, what's so special about being a photographer?

I began taking photographs when I was old enough to hold a camera. That's what my dad and my uncles did, so it seemed perfectly natural that I'd want to do it too. I loved looking at a photograph of Edward Weston's *Pepper* and would trace the curves and the shadows with my finger, liking the shades of gray and black though I didn't know exactly what I was looking at. Was it a body, without legs and head? I kept trying to figure it out, not even knowing what to ask.

We had large family gatherings with my mom talking and cooking, my dad behind the camera to record every possible moment. Before long that was me too, eye behind the camera, observing, waiting to capture the right moment, to grab the moment and keep it forever. I didn't have to tell anyone how uncomfortable it felt to have people looking at me, to answer the same questions over and over again: How is school? Do you like your teachers? What's your favorite subject? As if that's all a twelve-year-old thought about. Didn't they know that what I liked most was to be behind the camera, listening to their stories, wondering about their grown-up lives?

I observed and wrote poetry and stories about my grandmothers, how they came to America and made new lives for themselves, created families, had jobs. They told me stories about their mothers, who had been born almost one hundred years before me. I loved thinking of the threads that bound us all together. My grandmother Anne was the photographer in the family, lining up her six children on the stairs and recording every year of their lives with her Brownie camera. I have her photo albums now with little notes that say "someone's baby" or "Dad's cousin," names lost, but the photograph living on all these years later.

I was determined to be a writer, but when I went to college my dad suggested that I take a photography course "as a backup." Once in the darkroom, I decided that's where I wanted to be, among the hanging rolls of film, contact sheets, and smell of fixer. Unlike writing, where I had to start from a blank page every time, I could look through the camera lens and translate what I saw to film, then to paper. And I had something to talk about with my dad, something I could show to other people without laying my emotions bare. Something special.

But what's so special about it? Now I take photos with my phone most of the time, photos through car windows, snapshots on vacation, pictures to capture moments that I may not even print. What's the point? Anyone can do it. But can anyone do it the way I do it? Why does my photograph look different from yours? I've been told, "no one takes a photograph like you; no one has your eye." And that's what keeps me going.

Just as my life has sequenced from school to office, to raising sons, then back to office and leisure, my photographs have transitioned from middle distance (family portraits) to wide-angle (landscapes) and close-ups (flowers). I record what is closest to me. The big family gatherings are no longer, my children are grown, and what I have left are my surroundings, the mountains, the rivers, the gardens. My vision is both broad and detailed, focused on the world around me and the details that make up that world.

I remember the words of Martha Graham: "There is a vitality, a life force, an energy, a quickening that is translated through you into action, and because there is only one of you in all of time, this expression is unique.... You do not even have to believe in yourself or your work. You have to keep open and aware directly to the urges that motivate you. Keep the channel open." I'd like to say that I will keep the channel open and keep seeing the world only as I can.

We'll see what happens.

Julie Weinstein

A Responsibility to "Otherness": Considerations of the Use of Non-traditional Forms of Counseling with Refugees

Civil war, conflict, repressive regimes, and torture have potentially devastating psychological consequences for asylees, refugees, and internally displaced persons (IDPs). Up until the Bosnian war and then the genocide in Rwanda, humanitarian health assistance for refugees focused largely on the basic necessities of housing, nutrition, and sanitation. However, with the severe level of atrocities and the significant numbers of people involved in these conflagrations, mental health needs have become a priority. While this is an extremely positive and necessary development, concerns exist that the tendency to diagnose and treat asylees, refugees, and IDPs from a Western medically-oriented perspective, particularly with a diagnosis of Post-Traumatic Stress Disorder (PTSD), may create a culture of victims rather than survivors. Questions arise as to whether PTSD is always an appropriate diagnosis, whether traditional Western forms of therapeutic intervention are appropriate with people from non-Western and particularly more community-focused cultures, and whether non-traditional interventions can be therapeutic on their own and/or in concert with Western methodology.

Marjorie Muecke (1992) eloquently points out that "Refugees present perhaps the maximum example of the human capacity to survive despite the greatest losses and assaults on human identity and dignity" (520). How then, can we best help them to survive, and even thrive?

Gloria Jean Watkins, better known as "bell hooks" (2009), herself not a refugee but choosing, for a number of traumatic reasons, to leave her native state, wrote of feelings that appear to encompass and echo the feelings of loss and disconnect of many refugees. "I did not feel a sense of belonging…, I constantly felt like an unwanted outsider…. Digging in the California ground my hands touched earth, that was so different from the moist red and brown dirt of Kentucky…. I pondered the fact that traveling thousands of miles away from my native place had actually changed the very ground under my feet. Then I could not understand how the earth could be my witness in this strange land if it could not be a mirror into which I could see reflected the world of my ancestors, the landscape of my dreams. How could this new land hold me upright, provide me the certainty that the ground of my being was sound?" (12).

Refugee and IDP camps and host countries are home to hundreds of thousands of refugees who have fled the devastating effects of conflict and may be severely traumatized. UNHCR estimates that for 2011 there will be 10.4 million people living in refugee camps with an additional 4.7 million living in camps in the Middle East. Their 2008 estimate for people living in camps or settlements within their own country as IDPs was 26 million, with an additional 12 million people stateless in 2009. The total estimate by UNHCR for people forcibly displaced in 2011 is 43.7 million. A large majority of the people residing in camps or settlements who cannot go home and have been identified as needing asylum will remain there for the foreseeable future, as UNHCR estimates that only 10 out of every 100 refugees needing resettlement are settled each year (UNHCR Global Projected Resettlement Needs 2011, 2).

All too often, as the WHO *Rapid Assessment of Mental Health Needs of Refugees, Displaced and Other Populations Affected by Conflict and Post-Conflict Situations and Available Resources* notes, in "the field of health special emphasis has been put on nutrition, prevention, on management of infectious diseases, on maternal and child health. Much less attention has been given to mental health or to psychosocial needs" (1). Ensuring that basic needs are taken care of is, as Abraham Maslow (1968) points out through his Hierarchy of Needs, imperative as a base prior to other services being provided. However, refugees have been uprooted from their homes and possessions, seen people including family members killed, been separated from family and often cut off from their culture, been subject to "physical and psychological torture, shelling, sexual violence, and other atrocities" (Neuner, et al., 2004, 579). Many of

218

them need emotional healing, not only for their own sake, but for the sake of their families and communities and, indeed, for the well-being of the world.

Psychoanalyst D.W. Winnicott, in his theory about the mother-child relationship as key to infant growth and development, introduces the concept of "holding" wherein "the ego support of the maternal care enables the infant to live and develop" while she/he is in a state of dependence (586). Winnicott saw holding as literal—the actual physical holding of the infant—but also as figurative, as the provision of a safe and secure environment, both physiological and psychological, which would allow the infant to grow into a mentally healthy adult. This concept of "holding" was further applied by Winnicott and others to psychoanalysis with the analyst serving as an "emotional container" (Slochower, 710).

While the idea behind this concept is that the relationship between analyst and client is symbolic of the earlier mother-child relationship, we can also consider that any therapeutic relationship requires the holding of the client in a contained safe emotional space within which the therapist needs to constantly adapt to the particular needs of the individual client. This is particularly true for refugees, asylees, and IDPs who are all either still living in or have recently left unsafe space and need to be held within a safe space that allows them to heal from deeply traumatic events. How do we hold refugees, when we may never have been through anything like what they have experienced? How do we balance the needs of refugees with the needs of therapists who may themselves need assistance in being able to provide help in ways that are meaningful, when therapists may have strong motivation but also lack the necessary tools or understanding to best serve their clients who come from so many different worldviews?

It is all too easy for agencies of humanitarian aid to perceive refugees as sad homogenous groupings of victims of horrendous circumstances rather than as individuals, survivors with tremendous resourcefulness and resiliency. Not only may all survivors of a particular conflict or trauma be lumped together, but all survivors of all conflicts from all parts of the world including, among others, different cultures, ethnicities, beliefs, and religions, may be lumped together as similarly victimized and in need of the same therapeutic interventions. In this process, refugees can become identified with pathological labels which box them into particular categories of need and/or assistance. This impedes the ability of helping professionals to determine which people are truly in crisis and in need of psychological and perhaps psychiatric assistance from those people who may be resilient and relatively stable and need different forms of assistance.

Another aspect of the problems which can occur when refugees are labeled and lumped together is the possibility that, in our Western need to fit people into categories, we may also create circumstances where refugees are stigmatized, or at the least have the fear that they may be stigmatized, within their own communities. Douglas Raybeck (1986) looks at the concept of labeling theory where "because individuals are often linked to a significant number of co-residents through kinship and other interpersonal ties, attempts at labeling [can] result in social exclusion" (376), especially when people are labeled as "deviant" (which in many refugee societies includes diagnoses of mental illness). Gong-Guy et al. (1991) note that for refugees from Southeast Asian countries "all conditions requiring mental health treatment are highly stigmatized, and interventions are shunned" because mental health is seen as heritable and could damage an entire family's reputation as well as create problems for marriage for other family members. In addition, there may be fears that labeling could lead to deportation or, at the very least, the information would be made available to government agencies and spread throughout the refugee community (644).

Because of this potential stigma, one of two things may happen: People who do not need significant mental health assistance may be ostracized within their communities because they receive a label, or people who have been more seriously impacted by trauma and truly need help may be unwilling to come forward because of their fear of ostracism.

Of equal importance, lumping all refugees together reduces the degree of creativity available to helping professionals, impedes the ability of aid agencies to perceive refugees' resiliency as an aid to healing, as well as impedes their ability to see the potential helpfulness of and thus their ability to incorporate local helping professionals, and often excludes refugees from the possibility that alternative and culturally traditional forms of mental health assistance may be more, or additionally, efficacious in helping them to move forward with their lives. Renos Papadopoulos (2006) notes that when we look only at "the negative effects of trauma" we can "miss a great deal of other actual or potential responses that refugees have in relation to the adversities they had been exposed to" and we can deprive them of "the abilities that they themselves possess and which can be used in dealing with their predicament" (7).

Similarly concerned with the lumping together of refugees into internationally perceived categories of need and dysfunction without listening to their voices is Charles Watters (2001), who notes that "without an opportunity to articulate their own experiences in their own terms and to identify their own priorities in terms of service provision, refugees may be the subject of institutional responses that are influenced by stereotypes and the homogenizing of refugees into a single pathologized identity" (1710).

Lumping all refugees together creates the additional problem of believing that refugees in camps and refugees in host countries have similar types of issues. While they may have experienced similar kinds of traumas, Marsella et al. (1994) and Goodkind (2006) note that refugees in host countries have additional concerns that require an entirely different perspective on how to best help them. People in exile often face such new traumas as "lack of meaningful social roles, loss of community and social support, poverty and daily economic concerns about survival in a new country, marginal position/relative powerlessness in a new place, discrimination, lack of environmental mastery, undesired changes to their way of life, and social isolation" (Goodkind, 78). Marsella raises the concern that when refugees face such problems as "acculturation, racism, language, employment, housing, health, and personal safety" in host countries, for many of them, "the process of rebuilding their lives often proves to be as traumatic as the dislocation process from which they sought refuge" (5).

Additionally, if we perceive refugees based on our belief about what we feel people should be experiencing, the experiences we believe must have been most horrendous, what we believe we would feel under similar circumstances, or what we believe they need in order to heal, we provide no space for people's individual and unique experiences and worldview or the power of their emotional and spiritual capacity to heal themselves if we can provide them with the assistance that is appropriate for them.

Steven Reisner (2003) suggests that Western therapists and humanitarian aid organizations frequently bring with them images and assumptions about refugees which can end up with "the attempt to deter the survivors of traumatic circumstance from using their culturally familiar methods...when those methods clash with the values and fantasies of the therapists or the aid organization" (4).

Bracken et al. (1997) note that while helping professionals may consider torture to be the worst kind of atrocity, for refugees who have suffered numerous traumas "a torture experience will not necessarily be clearly separable from the other experiences, and some refugees have told us that torture was not the worst thing that had ever happened to them" (437). Kenneth Miller (1999) additionally expresses concern that while we may believe that the greatest trauma for refugees was exposure to violent events, it may be "a constellation of exile-related stressors such as the loss of one's community and social network, the loss of important life projects, changes in socioeconomic status and related concerns about economic survival, the loss of meaningful structure and activity in daily life, and the loss of meaningful social roles" that may be most traumatic (283).

Elaine F. Weiss

Reunion
June 9, 1982

As a loyal daughter of my dead Alma Mater, I too made the journey back. Attending the reunion of a college that no longer exists is the kind of peculiar experience for which there is no preparing.

There aren't many Kirkland College alumnae, and there can never be any more of us. Our college was founded in 1965 and passed into the realm of history by 1978. About 1200 of us Kirkland women are floating in the world, a tiny, finite species bound willy-nilly for extinction, but for one cold, rainy June weekend a good quarter of all our number gathered to celebrate what we'd once been.

In this season of college reunions, ours looked much like any other: There were banquets and parades, picnics, class photographs, fond embraces. There was a campus that used to be ours. There were grins, misty eyes, hilarious stories, and also a palpable pain.

"I fear I've outlived my college," said the young professional woman waiting on line at the reunion registration desk.

Under the circumstances, we did not want College Hill to look the same, but it did: lushly green, serene, and remote. Getting there still required the steady, twisty, mile-long climb up from the pretty village of Clinton (pop. 2000) which lies at the edge of New York state's Mohawk Valley, near Utica. On the left side of College Hill Road, the concrete and glass buildings of Kirkland still stood; on the right side of the road the stone and brick archways of Hamilton College.

Hamilton is a fine old liberal arts college, established in 1793, named for Alexander Hamilton and, until four years ago, a college for men. Kirkland was a college for women, named after a man (the founder of Hamilton, Reverend Samuel Kirkland, a missionary to the Oneida Indians) and brought into the world by Hamilton to be its helpmate. At a time when other men's colleges were "going co-ed" this new school would allow Hamilton to retain its size, masculinity, and demeanor yet still broaden its curriculum and bring women to its hilltop domain. (Years before, Alexander Woollcott, Class of 1909, singlehandedly overcame the absence of females at Hamilton by assuming all of the women's roles in student theater productions.)

The two schools lived together, side by side, "coordinate colleges" in the mold of Barnard and Columbia. They had their own presidents, faculties, and administrations and their own campuses, classrooms, and academic strengths but shared libraries and laboratories. Men and women students took classes on both sides of the road. The schools were very different in temperament: Hamilton was tradition-bound, ivy-

225

covered, and determined to prepare its men for the finest medical and law schools, for diplomatic and business careers. Kirkland was mercurial, feminist, eager to experiment, disdainful of conventional examinations and letter grading systems. Its hallowed halls were painted purple and yellow, and it encouraged its women to pursue their intellectual passions. That one school could have issued forth from the other was almost incredible, but they seemed to complement, to balance one another, and between them, the students on that Hill were offered an unusually rich educational experience.

But the 1960's and 1970's went by, the boom days of "innovative education" faded, economic and social conservatism took hold. So, when, upon entering its second decade, Kirkland asked Hamilton for a vote of confidence and a financial expression of faith, Hamilton decided it best to untie the cords of the coordinate arrangement and swallow Kirkland whole. The judgment was that a merger into one co-educational Hamilton would be more cost-efficient and convenient. The two Boards of Trustees and sibling administrations entered into a bitter struggle.

Students on both campuses protested, wearing shirts that read: "Living Together is Better Than Marriage." We alumnae held a protest vigil in New York City, in front of Rockefeller Plaza, linking arms with representatives of other women's colleges and selling apples (the Kirkland symbol) on Fifth Avenue. Nevertheless, the left side of College Hill Road is now called the Kirkland campus of Hamilton College, and stone pillars have been placed at the entryway, replacing the green and white Kirkland College sign.

We marched at the tail end of the Hamilton parade of classes, a processional slowly snaking its way from the steps of the white-steepled, Federal-style Hamilton chapel, across the quad, across the road, through the new stone pillars, and over to the Kirkland side. At the head of the parade were the men of the Class of 1912, and at the rear were the classes of the '70s, where we fit in. It was hard not to envy the Hamilton men, not for their class buttons or class hats or school ties, but simply for the length of their parade line, for the linear manifestation of their school's longevity and the comforting prospect of its continuing march through decades and generations and centuries.

Leading the parade was a hired band of bagpipers, and though we could barely hear the skirling from so far down the line, the sound of the pipes cheered us. The bagpipe was Kirkland's ceremonial instrument; we were piped into and out of every convocation and commencement for all our years. Kirkland used to bestow a Bagpipe Scholarship upon a talented women player, who then served as the official College Piper. A Scotsman may hear pipes and think of Culloden, but for a Kirkland woman, the sound of the pipes harkens her back to the blush of her college days.

A heavy drizzle fell upon us, and I pulled up the hood of my jacket to cover my head. For some of the women walking alongside me, such protection was not necessary, for they were already wearing their Kirkland hard hats. Wearing a construction hard hat is the ultimate mark of distinction for a Kirkland alumna—it shows you are a member of the Class of 1972, Kirkland's first graduating class. Called the Charter Class, they were hailed as "the pioneers," and we in the following classes always held them in awe and lived in their shadow.

They were brave women, that is for certain, and they didn't have it easy in paving the way. Their new college was not yet accredited—not yet built!—and almost all of their parents wished they'd chosen some other, more traditional, school. When they entered Kirkland in the fall of 1968 there was no campus, the land having only recently been an apple orchard and still a mess of mud and scaffolding. The academic structure and rules of the college were equally unformed, and there was a terrifying amount of trial and error ahead, but those fearless first Kirkies sat on endless ad-hoc committees, sat through turbulent governance meetings, and stood up to tell their professors a thing or two.

The hard hats were given to them during that tough freshwoman year by the Kirkland president, to thank them for helping to build the college. Their last names and first initials were written above the visors in white enamel, in the elegant hand of the president's wife. It's now been ten years since they wore those hard hats in their graduation ceremony. The photographs in the June 1972 issue of *Life* magazine showed them holding bunches of daisies, wearing long summery dresses instead of academic gowns, and their hard hats instead of mortarboards.

On this, the tenth reunion year of the Charter Class, the fourth year after what some of us call "the merger" and some of us call "the takeover" of our college, everyone who had ever studied, taught, or worked at Kirkland was invited back to the campus. Hamilton invited us. All through the winter and spring notices arrived in the mail, printed on facsimiles of the old college letterhead, bearing the Kirkland seal of a stylized apple tree, roots reaching down, limbs bearing its seed, flower, and fruit. Inside the oval border of the seal the name Kirkland was still printed at the top, but at the bottom, where it used to say "College" was substituted the word "Alumnae." We are the college now.

We were treated very well, handled with kid gloves. Emotions still run deep and wounds are still raw among those of us left without a college, so Hamilton went out of its way to make us feel at home, not just orphans invited to a family picnic.

We were given T-shirts and ceramic coffee mugs, printed with the emblem of our college and the phrase "Celebrate Kirkland." We were included in all the Hamilton Alumni weekend events, the cocktail parties and beer tents and dances, all of them bearing a frightening resemblance to the reunion scenes in Doonesbury comic strips. We were invited to join the Alumni Choir performance, and we did sing, even though the musical selections chosen by the choir director did not include any women's parts. We sang tenor.

Hamilton made dozens of earnest gestures of goodwill; the kind of delicate social diplomacy extended by a conquering nation to a vanquished one. Our name tags were handwritten in Kirkland green ink, and our dinner napkins were in a similar shade. At that dinner banquet, two huge ice sculptures—smooth tablets inscribed with the Kirkland seal drawn in green food coloring—decorated the room. With fresh white flowers gracing the base of the frozen tablets, the well-intentioned work of art did look distressingly like a set of Kirkland tombstones.

We were shown a documentary about ourselves, the work of a Hamilton woman student, who used old film footage, still photos, and recorded speeches to capture the spirit of Kirkland's early years. Kirkland only had early years. Accompanying the flash of pictures on the screen we heard the precise diction of Millicent Carey

McIntosh, the long-time president of Barnard College and then a founding trustee of Kirkland, extolling the virtues of a women's college education. (Dr. McIntosh had climbed into the cab of a bulldozer to break ground for the campus.) Her ringing words were followed by the baritone of Kirkland's idealistic young president, Samuel Fisher Babbitt, exhorting us to use our liberal arts educations to meet the challenge of the times. It was a time of riots and war.

The film, though highly complimentary, made us uneasy. We'd all seen this style of documentary before: sincere words spoken in hopeful tones, coupled with sunlit scenes of new beginning and endless promise — and it had the same heavy air of foreboding that those chronicles of the Kennedys do. It was also becoming clear that our time on College Hill, the Kirkland Years, had already become the stuff of legend among the present students, afforded a sort of dark, mythological status.

Asked to describe her college in one word, the Kirkland alumna wrote: Gone.

We had a meeting of our Alumnae Association. Our association lives on, after the demise of the college, in the hearts of a dedicated cadre of volunteers and in a post office box in Grand Central Station. In a Kirkland auditorium called the Red Pit, we discussed such existential agenda questions as: "Why should we still exist?" We took a vote to determine if our association should still exist, and a unanimous show of hands said "yes." Then we debated whether we ought to feel some responsibility towards helping the Hamilton women students. We argued whether our sisterly loyalties rightfully belonged to the co-eds on this Hill or to students carrying on the tradition of women's colleges (not too many of those left) or progressive education (also a dying breed) elsewhere. The role of alumnae-in-exile is a confusing one.

"Sometimes, when people ask me where I went to college," the Kirkland alumna explained, "I say: Atlantis."

Our last evening together we had a great, joyous bash and lots of Kirkland folks came—our deans and professors, secretaries and staff, even Joe, the chief custodian, to whom we gave a standing ovation. Absent from the festivities was a central charismatic figure in Kirkland's brief history, its first and only president, Samuel Babbitt. A rare closeness was formed between Babbitt and Kirkland students, especially the ones in the first classes, the kind of bond that having a common dream forges. But Babbitt declined the invitation to the reunion, lest his presence strain the fragile basting stitches of this attempted reconciliation with Hamilton. We alumnae were housed in the newly named Babbitt dormitory. His name was history, too.

But Babbitt sent a message to be read to us at the gathering: "You are not children of a different time, of an aberration called the '70s," he wrote. "You are gifted, fortunate deviants with a role to play in this or any time."

We passed around a book with blank white pages and each of us took a page, writing a message to be carried back to Babbitt, letting him know that we are surgeons, architects, dancers, and writers; we are businesswomen, teachers, weavers, lawyers, and mothers. Telling him, as we were telling ourselves, that we are succeeding, and that the college we built together did not fail us.

Elisabeth Weiss

It's Eventual

"It's eventual. It will happen." These words drift out the window to where Massachusetts Bay waves peak and flow. I came to this small town because of its beauty. Because it was what everything I came from wasn't. The sun's done with its fierce red announcement over the edge where water disappears into sky. "That's the place," my Polish grandfather told me, "where I come from." I think of this always. He never went back. He never spoke Polish again. What is it like to lose your language? Your home?

My mother is losing all of her memories. Sometimes I pick them up from around the house. I bring her a big basket of them: photos, jewelry, her honeymooning self on the rocks of Lake George, our dead pug's beaver coat which she stitched. Maybe she'll remember she was whimsical, loved a good joke as well as her beer straight out of the bottle.

I remember growing up in Staten Island, New York, where I was asked by the boys who pumped my gas down on Victory and Clove, by the kids at school, "Where are you from? What are you?" I look out to the horizon now, and I realize I have no idea.

When she first started to forget, we listened to *Porgy and Bess* in the evenings to calm down from the frantic days. Knowing she was losing her memories made her tight with fear, made her circle the dates on every page of each day's *New York Times.* Running from room to room, she gathered bankbooks, checks, and spread out the rainbow of passbooks holding the certificates of deposits she had squirreled away in banks all over New York City. There were so many dates to remember, to rollover, to collect. She arrived with one pair of pajamas and one bra. "I came for a vacation and decided to stay," she explained to anyone who questioned when she would be returning home.

But she did return home after a year. I lost her to Staten Island, to the dark house on the hill, the house of cards where Helena, a Polish caregiver, lifts her from her chair and props her in bed, like a rag doll. My mother's muscles have atrophied. She won't get them back. But meanwhile, there are pierogis, blintzes, stuffed cabbage, and soup, classical music to fall asleep to, and my father across the table. Some days she forgets how to chew. Other days she cries because she has forgotten herself.

In 1954 my parents left the Greenwich Village friendships of poets and painters for an island where they were friendless. What were they thinking? What did they want to give us, their eventual children? Maybe trees, maybe a safe path in the woods to walk to school. So, this is what it takes to become an adult, to choose what to give up. My mother stopped painting. She never made friends; nervous and determined, she joined a few groups, but they always petered out. Weekends we would go to Al Deppe's where for a few dollars we could all dine on hotdogs and hamburgers. Afterward, my sisters and I would run past the Skeeball machines to the back where chickens danced, where you recorded your own voice on 45s and you could ride in a rocket and watch the clown on a string dangle his painted limbs in merriment and joy.

The island has the largest garbage dump in the world. After the World Trade Center collapsed, all the debris was trucked down the Staten Island Expressway to the Fresh Kills Landfill. There they combed through it, uncovering DNA in miniscule bits of bone, jewelry, and fabric from clothing, things that fell through the white soot-filled sky. Concord Fire Station on Clove Road lost all but two men in the disaster. Each time I visit, I pass their memory garden on the way to the pharmacy to pick up my mother's medication.

The day the buildings fell, the phones went out. We frantically kept dialing. "Worse than anything I saw in the war," my father said when the circuits were reinstated. For years we watched the towers go up, excited about the newest, tallest building in New York. When my father was small it was the Flatiron Building on 23rd. Then it was the Empire State where a mynah bird bit my sister Ruth's finger because she stuck it in the cage. Then, in the early '70s, we were getting another, better version of how men could claim the sky.

The Verrazano Bridge, the largest suspension bridge in the world, completed a decade earlier, looked like a string of pearls at night. It brought a constant hum of traffic below my leaky casement windows. I tried hard to imagine a flowing river so that I could sleep. I never could. The bridge opened the island to Brooklyn residents who flocked to become homeowners. After the bridge, everything fell apart. My father crashed his car over a cliff

234

and landed upside down on someone's roof. He walked away, cat that he is, all nine lives intact except with broken ribs and ankle, and missing teeth. All the Staten Island planning boards sold out, and regulations went out the window. Builders and contractors moved in and took over almost every inch of open land, putting fill in the swamps and creating ticky-tack developments where all the houses on the block were identical. Despite this influx, hope loomed in the skeletons of the cranes on top of the World Trade Center, hanging over the island's horizon, like some imagined future promise, a world not unlike that in *The Jetsons* cartoon, of what we could become.

Before the bridge, we all lived in tiny hamlets. We didn't mix too much. The buses were slow. The SIRT train went over swamp and Little League fields. My husband's grandfather delivered newspapers with a horse and buggy in Tottenville and then later opened Flaxman's Department Store on Amboy Road. Each hamlet had a downtown for coffee shops and commerce. So, there was always a place for a parade on the 4th of July. The Boy Scout and Girl Scout troops could march and show off their earned badges and their skinned knees healed to shiny scars from all those hikes through High Rock Park, all those oaks and thorns and poison ivy patches that covered our island. When I tell people where I'm from they say, "What? People really live there?".

Now that I go back every month to visit, I've been thinking about what this island is, this place I'm from. Sitting in A Pig's Eye on Derby Street in Salem the other night, my husband I recollected vaguely from our childhoods, the odd and old Staten Island community of Sandy Ground in the hamlet of Rossville. The abandoned and hardly known geography of my childhood included that place, both exotic and known as well as Spanish Camp, the Conference House, Snug Harbor, Richmondtown, and Seaview. But it was Sandy Ground that we Googled that night, racing to see who could find it first. I still remember the open land of the earliest community of freed black slaves. I'm reminded it was settled in the 1830s by oyster fishermen from Delaware and Maryland. The Rossville AME Zion Church, active since 1850, was an important stop on the Underground Railroad, and some descendants still worship there today.

I also learned that Sandy Ground was once called Old Blazing Star. It lies close to The Blazing Star Burial Ground on Arthur Kill Road near Huguenot Avenue, with graves from the early 18th century. Nearby, a tugboat graveyard full of half-submerged vessels fills the Arthur Kill. It lies near the Kill Van Kull where a high school friend's body washed up one day.

I read how "The New York Public Library says hunting points dating from the end of the Ice Age were found in Rossville, and an American Indian campfire site was found in nearby Clay Pit Ponds Park" (Lanahan, 39). The English settled Rossville before the Revolution, according to the *Encyclopedia of New York City*, when the Blazing Star ferry transported its passengers to Woodbridge Township, New Jersey, over the Arthur Kill. Farmers thrived in the area, and the addition of a hotel in the 1880s briefly turned it into a resort (39). It's difficult to see Staten Island as a vacation spot as we drive down Rossville Avenue looking for the small museum dedicated to the original Sandy Grounds residents. Further along the road, "two abandoned gas tanks dwarf the Crazy Goat Feeds store, and Mollie Ryan's Public House overlooks the water" (14). We finally find the museum in a small development house, but it's closed for the season.

236

Thought to be sacred ground, Sandy Ground sustained many losses. First, the city condemned the oyster beds early in the 20th century because of pollution. Then many residents lost their homes to a 1963 fire (41). I was five years old at the time, in kindergarten at the Clove Valley School, P.S. 35 in Sunnyside. It was the same year Beth Esner, school monitor for the day, came in to tell us that President Kennedy was shot and we learned the word "evaporation" by leaving a jar of water on a sill for a week.

My father always loved history, and I loved the stories, glossing over the facts, which made me numb-brained and bored. My husband, a musician wannabe, always pointed out to our sons that for a song to be good you must always be able to hear the romance. I go back to Staten Island to find the romance, despite the garbage dump and the graffiti over the abandoned overpasses which stopped being built when the Staten Island Greenbelt was saved and where the Shack Boys found the perfect vantage point to watch a full moon rise. But that's another story. I return to find traces of myself, scraps in a heap, to hear the wings of pheasants in the briar release just before they fly, before the highway settles into my bones and the drone in my ears becomes commonplace, ordinary.

Nancy Avery Dafoe
and Jo Pitkin

My Favorite Years:
An Interview with
Dr. William Rosenfeld,
Author and One of the Earliest
Undergraduate Creative Writing
Program Directors

You know it is going to be a memorable interview when the film *My Favorite Year*—in which an aging, drunken, Peter O'Toole character sweeps across the screen in all his swashbuckling, absurd glory—comes up even before you ask a question. That is where William Rosenfeld, Marjorie and Robert W. McEwen Professor of English Emeritus and former member of the faculties of Kirkland and Hamilton colleges, wanted to begin—with broad wit, politics, romantic, aging idols, and absurdity. We

238

suspected there was a correlation to the early years at Kirkland. *

Kirkland College was the last-founded private women's college in the United States. It was chartered in 1965, opened in 1968, and merged—under protest in some quarters—with its coordinate partner Hamilton College in 1978. In the few years of its existence, Kirkland pioneered a number of concentrations on the undergraduate level, including Media Studies, American Studies, and Creative Writing. With the merger, Hamilton absorbed much of Kirkland's innovative curricula, including the creative writing major.

As Professor Rosenfeld's former students, we had long thought of Bill as our idol—although a sober one who is also a master at understatement and irony—and realized that he must have felt more like a character in a grand comedy during his early years building the Creative Writing Program at Kirkland College in upstate New York. Rosenfeld was among the earliest in the United States to direct an undergraduate creative writing program.

As products of Kirkland's short-lived but influential existence, Jo Pitkin, K'78, and Nancy Dafoe, K'74, relished the opportunity to talk with Bill Rosenfeld in his home in Utica, New York, about those pioneering days—the tumultuous years near the end of the Vietnam War and the upheavals it brought—of navigating the relatively uncharted waters of the undergraduate Creative Writing degree, before the profusion of MFAs moved across the American collegiate landscape.

Since retiring from Hamilton College in 1995, Rosenfeld has published two books, *Garibaldi and Rio Grande do Sul's War of Independence from Brazil*—[in which he created] *The Memoirs of Luigi Rossetti, John Griggs, and Anita Garibaldi* (Branden Books, 2013), and

Margaret Tugar: The Extraordinary Teacher, Principal, and Community Leader of Herkimer, NY (Branden Books, 2014), both containing elements of creative non-fiction. He and his wife Irma have continued to write.

When we arrived at their home, Bill and Irma, a former professor as well as associate dean at Hamilton College, invited us in for coffee and bagels before we ventured into their study that holds two computer desks with competing manuscripts facing one another, Irma's historical novel and Bill's novel.

DAFOE: Why did you choose to come to Kirkland?

ROSENFELD: We (looks at Irma) always said the last place at which we wanted to teach was a small, exclusive, isolated college. You might say that the college chose us. So here we ended up! I must add: with few regrets. (They laugh.) Carl Beier, the original chairman of the arts division, hired me as a writer and participant in the inter-arts seminar at Kirkland College, an innovative program in its own right.

PITKIN: You were teaching creative writing in Ohio at the time?

ROSENFELD: In the English Department at Baldwin-Wallace in Berea, Ohio, where I designed an inter-arts performance program—Arete—also quite innovative.

DAFOE: Beier hired you?

ROSENFELD: Again, Beier was the original chairman of the Arts Division, one of the four divisions at Kirkland College. The other three were Social Sciences, Science (principally history and philosophy of science), and Humanities. The Arts Division included Drama, Dance, Ceramics, Painting-sculpture, Music Composition and Theory, and Creative Writing. The entire program was guided into existence by President Sam Babbitt and under Millicent McIntosh's well-articulated vision. (She had been the President of Barnard College and was one of the principal forces behind the College's Advisory Committee.)

PITKIN: Who else joined the arts faculty when you did?

ROSENFELD: Buddy (Robert) Palusky**, in ceramics and sculpture. He built and set up the entire studio complex, pottery wheels, kilns, benches; he was a marvelous artist, who developed a technique for fusing glass and ceramics. I don't know if people realized how talented he was (still is), for he never advertised his accomplishments. Bobby won a top prize among international competitors in a Japanese invitational exhibition. Let me show you something. [He retreated from the room and returned with a huge ceramic vase with a Kewpie doll figure on the lid.] Bobby's sense of humor [Irma and Bill laughed]. When our daughter, Nina, was born, Buddy made this for her. Irma, who obviously also came when I did, taught a section of the inter-arts seminar.

Mordecai Sheinkman came earlier with Carl. He taught musical composition and theory. Peter Ostuni, a painter and sculptor, was here earlier also. And we had professional modern dancers and visiting theatrical directors. All practicing professionals. It was wonderful teaching in the same division with these artists.

DAFOE: How was Kirkland's program set up?

ROSENFELD: In addition to our specialties, we all taught sections in the inter-arts seminar, each of us bringing our own expert guests to the college to address all the students in the various seminars gathered as one audience. Quite unorthodox. I, for example, brought in a physical chemist as a visiting lecturer, Terry Cole of CalTech, who had the talent of illustrating aesthetic connections between scientific and artistic metaphors.

Kirkland College brought the Arts as a serious and coordinate discipline to the Hamilton College community of learning. By the calendar, Kirkland opened in '68, and some of us came in '69. The arts in particular formed quite a harmonious community. Of course, the Hamilton administration and faculty expected us to prove our legitimacy in an academic setting. As a result, like others, I found myself in some challenging, coordinating committees for the purpose of doing just that. In the face of feeling my way through those challenges, I frequently asked myself, what am I doing here?

Remember, at the end of the 60s, Creative Writing as a degree major was basically non-existent; hence the debate over the role of the arts as equal to the sciences, humanities, and social sciences prevailed. There weren't many models for creative writing programs, for example. The Iowa Writers' Workshop, of course, was well established, but almost no precedents existed for creative writing as an independent, undergraduate discipline. Look at it today!

DAFOE: I feel like we're still having this debate. The movement toward STEM schools in high school, even colleges feeling this pressure.

PITKIN: What kind of texts did you use in the courses?

242

ROSENFELD: No textbooks as such to teach Creative Writing existed, certainly none of value, as far as I could judge. I used collections of short stories and segments of novels to illustrate techniques developed by established writers. I designed a series of exercises for developing characters, their settings, and the evolution of their careers, that sort of aid.

PITKIN: What about the structure of the concentration in creative writing?

ROSENFELD: The Creative Writing program required a minimum of six workshops, including the Senior Writing Project, which was an independent study, but students had to take courses in the other divisions as well: science, humanities, and social sciences.

PITKIN: Yes, I remember arguing with you about that because I only wanted to take writing seminars, but you talked me into taking science and others.

ROSENFELD: A history of science course, at least one such. A writer has to have experience, draw from other systems of thought, as well as something in addition to personal experience to write about! ***

DAFOE: How did you determine pedagogical approach? I have wondered about this, as a teacher.

ROSENFELD: You teach creative writing, I recall.

DAFOE: I taught it for 16 years. How did you frame the program?

ROSENFELD: By feeling my way. I always looked at the question of what students needed in addition to a lot of actual practice in writing. I followed four practices around which I structured the workshops: First, every student had to take a turn at being a critic and at leading the rest of the class in criticism of a member's work. Second, when you had a piece being critiqued in class, you were to sit and listen without responding. Students resisted that part: listening to others' reactions because they wanted to give a defense or explain their intentions before they heard their classmates' comments. Third, after the views of all others were presented, then the writer could respond. And fourth, within a week of having her work criticized in class, each student had to meet with me so that I could give my observations.

DAFOE: I remember that well. What principles guided class criticism?

ROSENFELD: In your critique of your classmates' work, you had to be guided by how you could help the writer improve her work, how to realize her intentions. And probably most important, how you can help the writer develop honest self-criticism.

PITKIN: How successful were those early workshop classes?

ROSENFELD: I hope the Kirkland workshops were helpful for the writers. No one came out of a workshop without being much more aware of what she was doing— intending—than before. Allow me to refer to my own classes for a moment. I had a reputation as a technician.

244

I wanted members to shape their works with self-awareness, to be fully aware of the technique they developed toward establishing characters, their motives and responses to the complications that entered their lives, all within settings appropriate to their experiences. I wanted them to take their characters' lives apart, to examine their environments, and make them appropriate to their characters' development. My own background and training in literary studies played its part in my role as a critic and guide—and writer.

DAFOE: Could we return to a discussion of technique? Because it seems invaluable for students to be able to fully understand writing, the process of selection, choice, recognition, which we might substitute for the term technique, before producing a piece of their own.

ROSENFELD: Well, you are absolutely right, of course. But we should admit that there are some writers, some poets you simply can't analyze with any justice. How did Yeats come up with the line "I hear it in the deep heart's core" (from "The Lake Isle of Innisfree")? Should we sit around and speculate: Did Yeats first try, "the heart's deep core" or the "heart's core deep" before he arrived at that kind of perfection? (Laughs) There are just some writers— Keats, Dickinson, Sexton, Yeats, Shakespeare, Bishop— with whom that kind of manipulation and instinct are unfathomable. But we must try, anyway, to approximate their finesse, come as close as we can, and then try to emulate their best—what?—decisions. (In that regard, have a look at Yeats's "Adam's Curse.") Other than that, I can add little to your observations.

245

PITKIN: What surprises did you experience teaching Creative Writing?

ROSENFELD: I learned that when the students took Creative Writing, the quality of their compositions or expository techniques improved.

PITKIN: Did you have a favorite assignment, one that worked with all students?

ROSENFELD: Well, it's hard to think of assignments that worked equally well for all students. There were some assignments that helped most students develop ideas readily into stories or poems, but not every assignment meets every student's needs. As I recall, assignments in magic realism were generally effective. There is an early magic realism anthology, one of the earliest—that was wonderfully stimulating. One such assignment that I found widely successful called for students to transform their central character into an object she was handling, apparently mindlessly, but which was intimate to the character 's musing—the concept worked very well for most. Let me see, it called for the writer to start out with an incidental object, transform that object into a metaphor and then enlarge the metaphor into what becomes the character's reality. For example, a cup and saucer in a wife's hands become the object-stimulus; the wife's legs take on the shape of the saucer, her body becomes the body of the cup, the cup's handles become her arms; the whole person, in other words, is transformed into the ordinary object of utility that her family uses without thinking; i.e., they stop separating the woman from her commonplace functions in the home. Or, in another example, the character becomes a handsome tree in the woodlot behind the house. Her feet take root in the rich humus soil, her body holds her firmly upright, her branches, twigs, and leaves become limbs that sway to the rhythmic freedom of the refreshing breeze. She escapes ordinary reality into the freedom of the classic zephyr. She leaves all routine concerns behind. She becomes liberated from all onlookers, their cares, the expectations they place upon her.

PITKIN: I want to use that.

DAFOE: Do you see yourself as a writer or teacher first?

ROSENFELD: I never thought of myself as a writer but rather as a reader who might help writers become more proficient.

DAFOE: I always thought of you as a writer first and then my teacher.

ROSENFELD: That's interesting because it is so difficult to see how others perceive you at a given moment or context in one's relationship.

PITKIN: Of the various writers who taught at Kirkland, did they see themselves more as writers or teachers?

ROSENFELD: Oh, I don't know. They were all wonderful writers. Natalie Babbitt is still a writer and her class filled up fast, but she only taught the one course, in addition to which she carried independent studies with select students. That was the context for her most effective work. Carl Beier taught poetry, too, Michael Burkard and

Tess Gallagher are now established poets. And Jo, you had Michael and Tess.

PITKIN: Yes, and I just read their poems that appear in *Lost Orchard* at a reading during our all-Kirkland reunion.

ROSENFELD: Naomi Lazard and Kathy (Saltonstall) Dewart, also—Kathy, in particular, I think was an especially effective and conscientious teacher. Then Denise Levertov—whom I hired for one year; she saw herself as a guest writer primarily, but she was a memorable teacher.

PITKIN: And you brought in poets for single readings.

ROSENFELD: We brought in notable poets—Ciaran Carson, David Ignatow, Thomas Lux, W.D. Snodgrass, Stanley Plumley, Michael Waters, Robert Creeley, Carolyn Kizer, several others.

PITKIN: When I was preparing to moderate a panel at the AWP Conference in 2014, you told me that Kirkland was one of the early institutional members of AWP (Association of Writers and Writing Programs), right, encouraging those kinds of connections back then.

ROSENFELD: Naomi Lazard and I, as representatives of Kirkland, attended the very first AWP conference in 1972 at the Library of Congress in Washington, DC. That conference, as I recall, lasted two days! The entire membership of AWP could fit in one auditorium, and there were just two panels—one fiction and one poetry. Both panels included well-established writers.

DAFOE: Any issues you see now with the early writing workshop model?

ROSENFELD: Initially, everyone tended to be too soft on one another's work, but eventually participants became more hard-nosed and began to give more valuable criticism, the sort they hoped they would receive about their own work. For some students, particularly those who had always been told by their high school teachers that everything they wrote was promising, at the least, even polished, for those, the treatment they received in the Kirkland workshops was too discouraging. Some gave up or left the program. Many of them may have gone on to become successful writers on their own. I hope so. Others, knowing how hard they had to work to shape a story, for example, turned to other arts where perhaps they could enjoy more immediate satisfaction.

DAFOE: Looking back, would you have made any changes to your approach?

ROSENFELD: I may have had students read too many of the great authors' works as models—from what we now call the canon. As guides, those might have been too discouraging. Today, I might require readings from a wider range of genres. For some, there is value in emulating writers who find success in popular genres, those who produce a well-plotted piece with engaging characters and plots. In other words, I wish I had the students read the stuff that really sells, as well as in works that qualify as high art, as they are often called.

DAFOE: How did Hamilton react to those early days of Kirkland's opening?

ROSENFELD: Many members of the Hamilton faculty and administration were skeptical. You could not untie the knots of traditional attitudes. They didn't know what to make of Kirkland, and several among them fought it. Later, they embraced creative writing, of course. By the time I was tenured over to Hamilton, a few Hamilton people wanted to teach creative writing, but the program was already adopted as part of the English Department's offerings. I might add that after the merger, the workshops always filled to capacity, as they had at Kirkland.

PITKIN: Did you talk with the Hamilton faculty about how to teach Creative Writing?

ROSENFELD: I never tried to tell other faculty members how to teach a course in creative writing. When asked, I always tried to give helpful advice. There were some who wanted to know the details of my curriculum day by day. One colleague asked me, "How do you teach creative writing?" (Shakes his head) I told him, "If you really want to teach it, you can, with some guidance, develop an effective course."

DAFOE: Finally, how did you see the difference between those early Kirkland students and the Hamilton students you taught later (after Kirkland was annexed)?

ROSENFELD: Of course, from the beginning, we had cross-registration at the colleges. So, every Kirkland workshop included Hamilton students, eager and productive writers from both sides of College Hill Road. Institutionally, however, Hamilton saw the creative writing process

250

differently. Their focus was on how the writing could help them in another discipline, especially literary criticism. Other than that, most of the Hamilton faculty either tolerated or ignored the creative writing offerings (until the merger that is).

The Kirkland distinction, however, was that students took themselves seriously as writers, first and finally. They all wanted and expected to succeed. Let's back up here. As a teacher, I always took students seriously. If anything drove me, it was that: taking students seriously. Now, neither of you asked me this, but as a teacher at Kirkland, I found myself dealing with students who were better writers than I, better than I would ever be. There you have it. Now, if that ain't enough to wake one up, enough to characterize creative writing at Kirkland College, I'll drink my ink!

***

Just as Benjy Stone had his favorite year with the maddening, charismatic matinee idol Alex Swann, Kirkland's alumnae and faculty shared a bond that few in academia do today: together, they built a college, with all the exhilaration and frustration that the experience of forging something brand new brings with it.

*Kirkland President Samuel Babbitt details the early tumult and difficulties of balancing the divergent interests and politics of the day in his book about Kirkland College: *Limited Engagement: Kirkland College 1965-1978: An Intimate History of the Rise and Fall of a Coordinate College for Women*.

**Robert "Buddy" or "Bobby" Palusky taught ceramics and pottery at Kirkland College from 1969 to 1978.
***Jo Pitkin did take at least two history of science courses with Nadine George and Ruth Rinard, both fabulous Kirkland professors. Bill, her advisor, won.

M. Lori Richard Reidel

The Kirkland Legacy Lives on in Us and on the Hill

Why do I care about the Kirkland Legacy? Good question!

In 1978, Kirkland merged with Hamilton College. Although that was a real end for our college, our presence and reality took on a new form that has accomplished something meaningful and no less concrete: an imprint of us and our college that extends from the past to the present—and into the future as well. While it might be very easy for us alumnae to dwell in the past, the men and women of Hamilton College need to remember who we were, and are, and recognize Kirkland's major role in making their College the radically wonderful liberal arts college it is today.

So many Kirkland women, along with the amazing and supportive staff of the College, have worked together to ensure that the Kirkland College Legacy continues. Numerous dedications and personal involvements have occurred through the years and more are happening all the time, as we express our gratitude to our beloved

253

college and our dedication to keeping its spirit alive. What follows are just a few examples.

Dedicated in 2002, The Kirkland Gate is a flowing, green metal entryway into the creativity of what was, is, and always will be Kirkland College. Anonymously donated, with guidance and encouragement from Dick Tantillo, Vice President of Communications and Development, it was designed by John von Bergen, Class of 1963, and Ava Stein Bromberg, Class of 2002. Many were present for the dedication including our dear friend and fellow alumna, Susan Skerritt, K'77. And, yes, it was Susan who made the subtle yet strikingly beautiful Kirkland presence in this sculpture a reality. Since then, Susan has revealed herself as the donor as well. Through the years, she has lovingly carried our Kirkland banner. Our legacy is stronger as a result of Susan's opening door to all of us when we return to our Kirkland College campus.

The Pioneer Legacy Poster Project is an ongoing initiative, telling the varied, personal, and diverse narratives of Kirkland women. First publicly shared in 2012, the project assembles glimpses into our Kirkland lives. Paired with our past and current photos, these self-portraits are narratives of how our identities were formed, read, written, painted, kiln-fired, photographed, performed, and sung during our years at Kirkland, what we took with us when we left, and who we are now. The initial vision of Judy Silverstein Gray, K'78, the project explains how our lives as a collective of pioneer Kirkland women changed the College and why her legacy matters.

The Kirkland Arts Challenge was inspired during a question-and-answer session in the summer of 2009. Sam Babbitt was asked about the Hill and changes to the Kirkland campus. He said that Kirkland was not about the

254

geography or buildings. For him, its identity was the women who went there. Inspired by Sam's words, Carol Travis Friscia, K'77, thought deeply about a lasting memorial for Kirkland women. She created the Kirkland Arts Challenge and, with a committee of Kirkland women, considered what might create a lasting inspiration. The result was our Kirkland Wall, located in the Kennedy Center for Theatre and Studio Arts, and was initially celebrated in June of 2015. Intentionally listed in no particular order, the 1,407 women who matriculated at Kirkland College remain a limited edition and a lasting inspiration. I am so moved by this monument and the efforts made to acknowledge and memorialize our steps along the Kirkland path. Our names on this monumental wall cause a definite visual moment for anyone who passes by. While there are no names to add to the Kirkland Wall, our Legacy will gracefully pass our presence on to future generations of women and men on the Hill.

After the All Kirkland Reunion in 2015, a group of Kirkland women began to brainstorm about what might welcome future Hamilton women of need to the Hill. Kate Faison Spencer, K'79, created discussion, energy, and the inspiring creativity that can emerge from Kirkland women in motion. Established in 2019, The Samuel and Natalie Babbitt Kirkland College Scholarship Fund offers scholarship funds in perpetuity to future independent, creative, and strong women of Hamilton.

The tributes that we and others have made, along with Kirkland Reunions and other, less formal events, ensure that we stay connected with one another and that the Kirkland Legacy will endure long into the future, a memory with a purpose: inspiration!

Kyandreia Jones

The Kirkland Legacy:
Reflections of a Darksider

Kirkland College's bold spirit is inextricably woven into the fabric of present-day Hamilton College. Yet, as a community, we struggle to fully communicate its history and realize its undeniable legacy. Some students know that Kirkland women fought against the merger of the two colleges but ultimately lost this battle. It is significant how these empowering women responded to this loss. Instead of allowing their history to dwindle and die out, these phenomenal movers and shakers decided to nurture the seed of their legacy with the women who have, who are, and who will continue to flourish under the same independence, excellence, and resilience of their predecessors.

Although the merger between Hamilton College and Kirkland took place in 1978, students still consider the college in two parts: Lightside and Darkside. The green Kirkland College sign in front of the Kirner-Johnson Building marks the beginning of the Darkside. However, the impact of the women's college exists beyond the physical. This incredible legacy lives inside the spirit of every person who graces the same ground once tread by the women of Kirkland College.

Looking back on my time at Hamilton College, I realize that the part of campus that used to be Kirkland College was the only place on campus that truly felt like home. I spent most of my college career in Darkside dorms. I lived in Major, Minor, and McIntosh (I will not get into my short-lived stint in Eells my sophomore year—that dorm is undeniably haunted). I adored the Darkside partly because it was home to Opus 1, where I consumed my weight in chocolate chip cookies, but mostly because of its artistry, architecture, and allure.

The Darkside is unique from the rest of the college. It stands out because of its big windows, open spaces, and egg-carton ceilings. It is also known for its creative inhabitants and intentional outcasts who do not necessarily subscribe to the strict routine and cliques found in Lightside culture. The Darkside is more laid back, more go-with-the-flow, and more kumbaya. Music can be heard throughout the Darkside, either emitting from the Hans H. Schambach Center, permeating through Opus 1, or blasting through the windows of impromptu hang-out sessions among friends. From its decorated cement walls to the Kevin and Karen Kennedy Center for Theatre and the Studio Arts, Darkside is also full of art, expression, and community.

Further, this beloved part of campus also represents a safe place where diverse members of the community feel most comfortable. Thus, the names of the two sides of campus have a whole other significance.

"Lightside" and "Darkside" inadvertently allude to the racial divide represented in the living quarters as well as the differences in architecture. Like the women's college, the Darkside serves as a refuge for those who are unapologetically themselves and for those who dare to use their differences to enrich themselves and the campus.

While at Hamilton, I had the honor of being a Kirkland Scholar. My Posse mentor, Associate Professor of Philosophy Katheryn Doran, nominated all six women in our Posse for this scholarship. The scholarship recognizes students who demonstrate a commitment to the needs and interests of women on campus. During my senior year, I also applied for the Kirkland Endowment Fund (KEAC) to finance a life-changing trip to Atlanta, Georgia, with Associate Professor of Literature Pavitra Sundar and Phinix Knight-Jacks, H '19.

Though I understood how Kirkland influenced me personally, I was not aware of Kirkland's influence on Hamilton's academics. Until recently, I did not know that Kirkland's innovative curriculum allowed nontraditional disciplines like creative writing to exist at Hamilton. When I was a high school senior, Hamilton's emphasis on writing is what drew me to the school. As a Creative Writing major, I am grateful for the nontraditional curriculum that Hamilton inherited from Kirkland. The ability to express myself, others, and the world around me play a crucial role in my understanding of myself and my surroundings.

Whether advertently or inadvertently, Kirkland College and its alumnae have been an integral part of my life as both a student and as a graduate. For this reason, I, too, am proud to represent its immense legacy.

258

Kirkland in Pictures

"The Rock," a meeting place for Kirkland and Hamilton college students in McEwen Hall.
Courtesy Hamilton College

Class of 1975 graduation
Courtesy Hamilton College

MALVINA TSOUNAKIS ✏ MONIQUE OEI ✏
ELIZABETH MASON ✏ MARJORIE HOMON
ROBIN BECKER ✏ DEBBIE LERNER ✏ SUSA
AMY KRINSKY ✏ KATHRYN BLOCH ✏ RIS
CATHARINE PARK ✏ ELISABETH HORWITT
CORDELIA BURPEE ✏ MIRIAM HACK ✏ DUL
HELEN MOORE ✏ JANE DINEEN ✏ ROBE
SUSANNE MARCUS ✏ ESTHER SHAO ✏ NA
ISABEL WEINGER ✏ IJEAMAKA OTUE ✏ YV
CAROL BAKER ✏ SUZANNE SEMMES ✏ AN
AMY MARSTERS ✏ ANNE FRY ✏ KATHRYN B
ROSALIND CHAST ✏ SUSAN SPAGNOLI
SUSAN VALENTINE ✏ JUDITH STEINLAUF

Detail of the Kirkland College Wall at the Kennedy Center
for Theatre and Studio Arts
Courtesy Isabel Weinger Nielsen, K'76

The Kirkland gate at the entrance to the Kirkland College campus.
Courtesy Isabel Weinger Nielsen, K'76

Kirkland College historical sign
Courtesy Isabel Weinger Nielsen, K'76

Kirkland Class of 1974, 40th reunion, 2014
Courtesy Isabel Weinger Nielsen, K'76

Kirkland College Graduation 1977, a year before the merger of Kirkland and Hamilton Colleges.
Courtesy Hamilton College

Kirkland Class of 1976, at the all-Kirkland reunion
2007, wearing hard hats like the Kirkland Charter
class.
Courtesy Isabel Weinger Nielsen, K'76

Kirkland College alumnae authors' section at the
Hamilton Bookstore.
Courtesy Isabel Weinger Nielsen, K'76

Contributor Biographies

Barbara deB. Allen Purinton, K'71

Barbara (Bonnie) Allen Purinton graduated from Kirkland in 1971 with a BA in Government, the first woman to attend the Hamilton College Semester in Washington in 1970. She was ordained in the United Church of Christ and has served churches in Vermont since 1978. After 30 years of settled ministry, she worked with the Vermont Army National Guard Family Readiness program during the Afghanistan deployment of her husband and daughter. She currently serves as a full-time interim pastor, looking forward to retirement and more writing time. She and her husband Charlie live in North Hero, Vermont, and have three children and two grandchildren. Barbara has an MDiv from Andover Newton Theological School, a DMin from Palmer Seminary, and an MFA (2014) from Goddard College. She has been an EMT since 1990.

Ashton Applewhite, K'74

Author and activist Ashton Applewhite is the author, most recently, of *This Chair Rocks: A Manifesto Against Ageism*. Ashton has been recognized by *The New York Times*, *The New Yorker,* National Public Radio, and the American Society on Aging as an expert on ageism. She blogs at *This Chair Rocks*, has written for *Harper's*, the

Guardian, and *The New York Times*, and is the voice of *Yo, Is This Ageist?*. In 2016, she joined PBS site Next Avenue's annual list of 50 Influencers in Aging as their Influencer of the Year. Ashton speaks widely—until the pandemic, that is—at venues that have ranged from universities and community centers to the TED mainstage and the United Nations. She is a leading spokesperson for a movement to mobilize against discrimination on the basis of age.

Nancy Avery Dafoe, K'74
Author, poet, and English educator Nancy Avery Dafoe writes across genres and has ten published books. In addition to her Vena Goodwin murder mystery series, including *You Enter a Room*, *Both End in Speculation*, and *Murder on Ponte Vecchio*, Dafoe has written short stories and poems. Her poetry earned first place in the William Faulkner/Wisdom creative writing competition, and her short stories won first place in the New Century Writer competition. Other published books include *An Iceberg in Paradise: A Passage through Alzheimer's*, a memoir. She has also written textbooks on education and writing: *The Misdirection of Education Policy*, *Breaking Open the Box*, and *Writing Creatively*. She has two books of poetry, *Poets Diving in the Night* and *Innermost Sea*. Her novella *Naimah and Ajmal on Newton's Mountain* will be released in 2021. A former high school and community college English teacher, Dafoe lives in Homer, NY.

Natalie Babbitt
Natalie Babbitt (1932-2016) began her career by illustrating a book for children written by her husband Samuel Babbitt and edited by her only editor, Michael di Capua. She began writing illustrated stories in verse, but soon undertook her own prose works. She has published

268

15 books, often illustrating her work, and added drawings to nine books of verse by the poet Valerie Worth. *Tuck Everlasting* (1975), Babbitt's best-known book, has won significant acclaim. Translated into many languages, and adapted for stage and screen, it is used extensively in elementary schools, and was presented as a Broadway musical in 2016. Her book *The Eyes of Amaryllis* has also won awards. Her literature earned Babbitt the E.B. White Award, and she was the U.S. nominee for the international Hans Christian Andersen Award. Babbitt lectured at Kirkland.

Samuel Fisher Babbitt
Samuel Fisher Babbitt joined the Yale administration upon graduation in 1953. In 1957, he was appointed Dean of Men at Vanderbilt University, and in 1961, he briefly served in Washington as College and University Liaison for the Peace Corps. Completing his doctorate, Babbitt was appointed President of Kirkland College in 1965, where he served until the college was assimilated into a coed Hamilton in 1978. After heading fundraising at the Memorial Sloan-Kettering Cancer Center, Babbitt, became Vice President for Development at Brown University in 1983. Babbitt chronicled the brief history of Kirkland College in his book *Limited Engagement: Kirkland College 1965-1978, An Intimate History of the Rise and Fall of a Coordinate College for Women*. "Retiring" in 1992, Babbitt indulged a life-long interest by heading the Board of the Gamm Theatre, a small and vital Equity house. He was also active "on the Boards" over the next twenty years. Samuel Babbitt lives in Hamden, CT.

Rachel Dickinson, K'78

Rachel Dickinson has written extensively for numerous publications, including *The Atlantic, History Channel Magazine, National Geographic Traveler, Salon, Smithsonian, Catapult, Audubon, Aeon, Panoramic,* and *Yankee Magazine.* She holds a degree in geology from Kirkland and an MFA in creative nonfiction from Goucher. Currently working on her eighth book, Dickinson has the distinction of being Kirkland College's first and only recipient of a Thomas J. Watson Fellowship. Author of several books, including *Falconer on the Edge: A Man, His Birds, and the Vanishing Landscape of the American West* and *The Notorious Reno Gang: The Wild Story of the West's First Brotherhood of Thieves, Assassins, and Train Robbers,* she has also written several nonfiction books for middle-school children. Dickinson is currently working on a memoir in essays titled *The Loneliest Places* for the Three Hills imprint of Cornell University Press.

Margaret Doris, K'77

Margaret Doris graduated from Kirkland College with a concentration in American Studies (American History/American Religion). Her advisor was David Locke; other professors assisting in the development of her concentration were Bill Hoffa, Joel Tibbetts, Lafe Todd, and Mel Endy. She received an MDiv in pastoral theology and PhD in bioethics/Christian ethics from Boston University.

Linda Dunn, K'77 (cover art)

Linda Dunn received her BFA from the Rhode Island School of Design in 1991. She has worked as a file clerk, secretary, tech writer, sweater-designer, production seamstress, mother, and textile artist. She now paints and teaches art to adults, focusing on seniors in long-term care. "I am the daughter of a classical pianist and an engineer. With them in my heart, I encourage my students to improvise while they improve technique. Art-making involves craft; it also embraces not-knowing. When I create, my goal is visual music, in which elements converge to express the energy of our lives." Linda lives in Cambridge, MA, and is a member of the Loading Dock Gallery in Lowell, MA. Find her art on Instagram and at her website, LindaBranchDunn.com.

Carol Durst-Wertheim, K'73
Carol Durst-Wertheim has taught in culinary arts, food studies, hospitality, and tourism programs at several New York metropolitan universities. She was the first Director of the New York Restaurant School, owned New American Catering, wrote *Vignettes & Vinaigrettes: A Memoir of Catering before Food Was Hot* (2020) and *I Knew You Were Coming So I Baked a Cake* (1997), and completed an Oral History for the New York Women's Culinary Alliance (2013). She researched women's food industry work for her dissertation and is currently a board member and President of the Federated Conservationists of Westchester County and a former board member of Women Chefs and Restaurateurs (Mentoring Program) and Infinite Family, an on-line mentoring program for South African teens.

Stephanie Feuer, K'77
Stephanie Feuer is a New York City-based writer and marketing executive. Her work has appeared in *The New York Times*, *Slate*, NBC News *THINK*, *Narratively*, *The Billfold*, *Organic Life*, *The Forward*, and numerous anthologies. She is the author of a novel for young adults,

Drawing Amanda (HipsoMedia, 2014). For more than a decade she was a marketing executive at The New York Times Company. Stephanie started her career as a disc jockey and radio news reporter. She is currently working on a book about smell and memory which won the MIT Press Pitchfest. Find her at stephaniefeuer.com or @StephanieFeuer.

Doris Friedensohn

Doris Friedensohn was Dean of Students and Associate Professor of American Studies at Kirkland College from 1970 to 1973. Among her preoccupations at Kirkland were innovative education and social change. She is Professor Emerita of Women's Studies at New Jersey City University. After retiring, she published a food memoir; she also spent "a small lifetime" at the Food Service Training Academy of The Community FoodBank of New Jersey in Hillside, NJ. Her memoir *Eating As I Go: Scenes from America and Abroad* (2016) is about learning, teaching, and change, a consequence of her remarkable experiences. *Airports Are for Waiting: And Other Traveler's Tales* is Friedensohn's latest book (2019).

Elias Friedensohn

Elias Friedensohn (1924-1991) chaired the Arts Division at Kirkland from 1970-72. He was Professor Emeritus of Art at Queens College, CUNY, where he taught for almost 40 years. Friedensohn has had nearly 50 one-person shows, and his work has been collected by many U.S. museums. From his estate's website: "Friedensohn's voyage as a narrative artist encompasses interior worlds of anguish, fear, manic play and transcendent love; also, cityscapes, seascapes, exotic markets and late 20th century airports." During his lifetime, Friedensohn received many

272

awards for his art, including a Fulbright Grant and an award from the American Academy of Arts & Letters. For a more thorough overview, see the website www.eliasfriedensohn.com and the Newsletters (included on the site under "Musings") published by his Estate.

Jane Gottlieb, '80
Jane Gottlieb is a 1980 graduate of Kirkland-Hamilton who has worked as a journalist for many years in the Hudson Valley. She is a freelance writer based in Albany who contributes to many national and international publications. She is indebted to her college—even the one that ate up the other one—for helping her develop writing and communication skills. She may be reached at janerite@verizon.net.

Cassandra Harris-Lockwood, K'74
Cassandra was born in Washington, DC, and grew up in the Utica area. From an early age, she was very active in student government and social activism. She became the first female construction worker in New York State while at Kirkland. She graduated with a BA in Fine Arts and Dance. She worked for several years in New York City in performing, martial, and healing arts. She returned to the Utica area in 1979 to marry attorney Stephen L. Lockwood. In 2002 she founded For the Good, Inc. (FTG), a not-for-profit helping low-income Utica residents. FTG operates the Utica Community Gardening Initiative and the Study Buddy Club, which, in collaboration with Hamilton College, prepares Utica students for the Regents exam and for college, and also publishes the *Utica Phoenix* news magazine. Cassandra created the Oneida County Black History Archive with Dr. Jan

DeAmicis and the late Dr. Paul Young of Utica College in 2012. In 2018 the archive was donated to Hamilton College and is now part of the Burke Library's permanent collection. Also, in 2018, she created Phoenix Radio, Inc., where she hosts the *Hot Seat* Monday through Thursday. Cassandra and Stephen live on a small horse farm in Clinton, NY, with their two grown sons. Cassandra sings in the choir at St. Joseph - St. Patrick Church, practices natural healing and homeopathy, and is a guitarist and singer-songwriter.

Susan Hartman, K'74
Susan Hartman, an award-winning writer, was educated at Kirkland College and received an MFA from Columbia University. She has written cover stories and profiles from places as different as Northern Ireland and Queens, Las Vegas, and Brooklyn for *The New York Times*, *The Christian Science Monitor*, and *Newsday*, often following her subjects for months. Her book, *City of Refugees*, is forthcoming from Beacon Press. The author of two books of poetry, *Dumb Show* and *El Abogado*, she teaches in Columbia University's MFA writing program.

Martha Hawley, K'73
Martha Hawley was born to U.S.-Canadian parents, raised in New York suburbs, and is now a U.S.-Dutch dual national and resident of Amsterdam. Her 1973 Kirkland BA in Languages and Literature was earned on the Hill, in Bogotá, Colombia, and in New Haven (Modern Chinese at Yale). She has worked in radio production and currently writes narrative nonfiction, and has been published by *Carrillo Gil Museum*/Mexico; *IPS (Inter Press Service)*; *De Appel Bulletin, Mixed Magazine, Museumjournaal, NRC Handelsblad, oDrom International, Toneel Teatraal/*

Netherlands, *Silk Road*/ Taiwan, *Songlines*/ UK, and other European and North American publications. You can view some of her past radio works at radionetherlandsarchives.org/?s=Hawley.

Alice Hildebrand, K'73

Alice Aldrich Hildebrand grew up in New York and moved to Maine in 1978. In 1969, she received a National Council of Teachers of English Award for her poetry. At Kirkland, she worked with Denise Levertov and Naomi Lazard and received the Watrous Award for poetry. In 1976, she received the North Carolina Poetry Association award. Her stories and poetry have appeared in *Killick Stones* and *Puckerbrush Review*. In 1987, she won the Hampton's International Award for poetry. She has worked as a journalist and book reviewer. She graduated from Bangor Theological Seminary in 1987 and received Privilege of Call in the United Church of Christ in 2003. She is a Board Certified Chaplain who has worked in hospitals, in hospice and palliative care, and in pediatrics, and published articles on her research in the field of spiritual care. She is married and has three sons and four grandchildren.

Elisabeth Horwitt, K'73

Elisabeth Horwitt majored in creative writing and won a Watrous Prize for short fiction. Upon graduation, she moved to Cambridge and freelanced for such publications as *The Real Paper*, *The Boston Globe*, and *American Way*. Her first paid piece was for a local tabloid called *Chomp*, about the obstacles facing women who want to become chefs. In 1981, she became a staff reporter for *Business Computer Systems*, a monthly magazine geared to technophobic businesspeople. She went on to cover pre-Web data communications for *Computerworld*, then went freelance in order to concentrate on her son and fiction. She recently finished *Lucia and Susan*, a historical novel about Cambridge, MA.

Dorothy Irwin, K'76
Born in Georgetown, British Guiana (now Guyana), Dorothy Irwin has spent her career in the publishing industry, first with design studios producing educational books, then as copy chief for such magazines as *Saveur*, *Bon Appétit*, and, currently, *This Old House*. Her appreciation of the power of personal narrative to illuminate the past flourished during the ten years she worked with the editors of *American Heritage* magazine. She lives in Brooklyn, NY. In completing *Years of High Hopes*, she was assisted by several Guyanese, including Hamilton professor Nigel Westmaas, who graciously agreed to read and comment on the manuscript.

Abigail Johnson, K'75
Abby Johnson contributed to the Fresh Ideas opinion column in the Carson City *Nevada Appeal* with a group of progressive women from the column's inception in 1997 until 2019. This column was published on February 5, 2014. Nevada has been her home since 1980. She consults for rural local governments on community development, nuclear waste, environmental impacts, and public information. She is also the activist president of Great Basin Water Network, protecting water at its source.

Kyandreia Jones, '19
Kyandreia Jones is a Posse Miami Scholar and graduate of Hamilton College, where she received her BA in Creative

Writing. She was born and raised in South Florida. Kyandreia's poetry and prose have been published in *The Black List Journal*, *The Underground*, and *The Spectator*. She is also the author of two children's books: *Choose Your Own Adventure SPIES: James Armistead Lafayette* (2019) and *Choose Your Own Adventure SPIES: Mary Bowser* (2020). Kyandreia continues her career as a freelance writer, educator, and visiting author and has recently begun screenwriting in the hopes of writing for film and television.

Carol Kindig Urbanic, K'76
Kirkland's emphasis on writing, personal growth, responsibility and service made it unique. For me, Kirkland was an ideal educational experience: inspiring professors who supported and challenged us assessing our work not with grades but with often intense evaluation. In addition, my international "bent" and passion for other cultures and languages were nurtured, especially in anthropology. I earned my B.A. in Foreign languages at Kirkland. After college, I worked for the federal government and an international corporation, two universities, and a non-profit. But I'm even prouder of the volunteer work I did while raising our two wonderful children. I have volunteered extensively through our church, an international exchange program, and in our children's schools--in global competence and the fine arts. I am an internationalist, an eclectic, and well-rounded, life-long learner, and a passionate volunteer in large measure because of Kirkland .

Kathryn E. Livingston, K'75

Kathryn E. Livingston is the author of the memoir *Yin, Yang, Yogini: A Woman's Quest for Balance, Strength, and Inner Peace* (Open Road Media). This piece originally appeared on *The Huffington Post*. Kathryn and her husband Mitch live in Bergen County, NJ, where she spends most of her time writing, blogging, book reviewing, or teaching Kundalini yoga. She is working on a second memoir, *Torn Between Two Gurus*, and is represented by Amy M. Schiffman (K'77) of Echo Lake Entertainment. Visit Kathryn on Facebook, follow her on Twitter, or send her an email and let her know whether *your* kids have started calling all the shots.

Anne Mavor, K'74

Anne Mavor is an artist and writer based in Portland, OR. She combines storytelling, research, performance, visual imagery, and collaboration to illuminate social issues. Originally from Massachusetts, in 1976 she moved to Los Angeles to join the Feminist Studio Workshop at The Woman's Building. She received a grant from the John Anson Kittredge Fund for *Strong Hearts, Inspired Minds: 21 Artists who are Mothers tell their Stories*, published in 1996, and a writing residency from The Mesa Refuge. Since 2010, paintings from her Mounds and Stones series have been exhibited in Oregon, Washington, and Massachusetts. The touring installation *I Am My White Ancestors: Claiming the Legacy of Oppression* premiered in 2016 and has been supported by The Puffin Foundation, the Regional Arts and Culture Commission, and individual donations. Anne has a BA in art from Kirkland College and an MFA in creative writing from Antioch University, LA.

Patricia McLaughlin Amidon, K'72

Patricia McLaughlin Amidon applied to enter the charter class, even only if because "she had no clue." However, she was hooked on the idea of Kirkland when she read in the very first catalogue, "teaching was an exchange between an experienced learner and an inexperienced learner." She ultimately was on the "Seven-Year-Plan," quitting twice to "find herself" but eventually graduated in 1975. She currently lives on a boat with her husband, address left to the whims of the drift.

Helen Morse, K'76

Helen Morse was born in New York City in 1954. She attended Sarah Lawrence College for two years, then transferred to Kirkland where she graduated with a bachelor's degree in Fine Arts Photography. She has been active in many different fields, including museum work, children's theater, antiques, real estate, gallery sales, and sheltering the homeless. She is presently working on finishing a personal memoir. Her photographic work, which spans over 40 years, can be seen at helenmorse.com.

Ellen O' Brien, K'72

Ellen O'Brien is a member of Kirkland's Charter Class. After earning her PhD in English at Yale, she returned to Kirkland to teach. In 1978, she moved to Guilford College, where she taught for twenty-two years—first English and then theatre. She also began working with actors on speaking Shakespeare, and in 1993 earned Advanced and Post-Graduate Diplomas in Voice Studies from Central School of Speech and Drama, London. Since 2000, she has been Head of Voice and Text for the Shakespeare Theatre

Company and the Academy for Classical Acting in Washington, DC.

Gwynn O'Gara, K'73

Gwynn O'Gara is the author of five published chapbooks of poetry including *Sea Cradles, Winter at Green Haven, Fruit of Life, Fixer Upper,* and *Snake Woman Poems.* Her poems appear in numerous literary journals. A long-time California Poet in the Schools, O'Gara was also a Poet Laureate of Sonoma County, CA. She earned the National League of American Pen Women's 2019 Shirley Holden Helberg's Grant in Letters in 2019. O'Gara's book of poetry *Clio's Daughter, Girl with Head on Fire* was chosen from a large field of high-quality entries as a finalist in the Faulkner/ Wisdom poetry book competition. She lives in California with her husband Rob, a musician.

Jo Pitkin, K'78

Jo Pitkin is the author of *Cradle of the American Circus: Poems from Somers, New York; Commonplace Invasions; Rendering;* and *Village: Recession* and the editor of *Lost Orchard: Prose and Poetry from the Kirkland College Community.* Her poems have appeared in such journals and anthologies as *The New York Review of Books, Little Star, Salamander, Nimrod, A Slant of Light: Contemporary Women Writers of the Hudson Valley,* and *Raising Lilly Ledbetter: Women Poets Occupy the Workspace.* After working as an editor at Houghton Mifflin Company, Jo continues her career as a freelance educational writer for kindergarten through Grade 12 students. www.jopitkin.com

Joanne Rappaport, K'75

Joanne Rappaport is an anthropologist who teaches in the Department of Spanish and Portuguese at Georgetown University. Since her junior year at Kirkland, she has been conducting ethnographic research in southwestern Colombia with indigenous groups, as well as historical research in various archives. She is particularly interested in collaborative research methodologies that support grassroots organizing among indigenous peoples and peasants in Latin America, and has for several decades collaborated with various indigenous organizations in Colombia, training local activists to conduct their own research projects. Her book *Cowards Don't Make History* (Duke, 2020) was recently completed. She lives in Washington, DC, with her husband, David Gow, who is also an anthropologist. Her daughter Miriam Rappaport-Gow is a teacher in Washington, DC.

Douglas Raybeck

Douglas Raybeck is professor emeritus of anthropology at Hamilton College. He received his PhD in anthropology from Cornell University in 1975. He has published more than 60 papers and six books, four of which were co-authored. Topics have ranged from fieldwork in Kelantan, Malaysia, to psycholinguistics, to study skills, the likelihood of extraterrestrial intelligence, and future studies. His most recent book is *Looking Down the Road: A Systems Approach to Future Studies*.

M. Lori Richard Reidel, K'77

M. Lori Richard Reidel graduated from Kirkland College in 1977 with a BA in Studio Art. She is a Certified Advanced World Peace Yoga teacher, Reiki Master, and potter in

Cincinnati, Ohio. Learning about peaceful action, while juggling many varied and different projects during her studies at Kirkland, Lori created a path that continues through her joyful life. As President of Kirkland College's Alumnae Association since the fall of 2012, Lori enjoys building our community. Married to the poet and writer James Reidel, they have three sons, two daughters-in-law, and a beautiful granddaughter.

William Rosenfeld

William Rosenfeld joined the Kirkland faculty in 1969 and served through the merger, enjoying the rich and productive energy of the Kirkland people. During that time, he directed the program in creative writing and served as chair of the arts division, retiring in 1995. "Kirkland lives on in the continuing productivity of those wonderful writers," he said. Rosenfeld is the author of the novel *Garibaldi: The Memoirs of Luigi Rossetti, John Griggs, and Anita Garibaldi* (2013) and the nonfiction book *Margaret Tuger* (2014) about a Herkimer educational leader.

Deborah Ross, K'75

Deborah Ross, a native Utican, received her doctorate in English at University of Rochester in 1980 and then eventually became Professor of English at Hawaii Pacific University, studying the way gender shapes narrative from works such as Shakespeare and Jane Austen to Disney and Miyazaki. After two marriages she found herself raising two children in a strange environment, and saw how her own life was shaping her narrative. Her short story "Snakes" recently won third place in the Lorin Tarr Gill writing competition from the Hawaii chapter of Penwomen. A partial bibliography can be viewed at

282

Betty Sarvey Salek, K'78

Betty Sarvey Salek majored in Creative Writing and Literature at Kirkland. Following graduation, she worked at a newspaper as a reporter, editor, and photographer, and as mom to her daughter and twin sons. For the last twenty years, she has been a substitute teacher, giving her inspiration and time to write once again. An excerpt from her children's story *A Fish in the Mirror* appeared in *Lost Orchard*. Betty lives in a rural community near Clinton, NY, with her children nearby.

Amy Schiffman, K'77

At Kirkland, Amy Schiffman studied creative writing with Bill Rosenfeld and Kathy Saltonstall. For the past twenty-five years, she has worked as a literary agent in the motion picture and television fields and is currently a literary manager at Echo Lake Entertainment in Beverly Hills, specializing in representing adapted works. Notable recent projects include *The Guernsey Literary and Potato Peel Pie Society* (2018) and *Minamata* (2020). Before coming to Los Angeles, she was a magazine columnist and editor at *Diversion*, *GQ*, and the award-winning *American Photographer* magazine. Her essay "The Last Ten Years" appeared in the first volume of *Lost Orchard*. Inspired by that experience of being published with her alumni peers, she is currently at work on a novel.

Jan Sidebotham, '79

Jan Sidebotham graduated from Hamilton in 1979 after three years at Kirkland. She taught English in private middle and high schools in Washington, DC, and then

Brookline, MA. She left teaching in November 2015 for Cape Cod, where she paints and does free-lance tutoring. She wrote a bi-weekly column for *The Spectator* in her junior and senior years. She delivered a speech at the first co-ed Hamilton College commencement, hoping to use the opportunity to honor the many Kirkland professors who were unrecognized and under-appreciated during the Big Gulp, such as George Bahlke, David Miller (Religion), Carol Rupprecht, Stephen Lippman, Sybille Colby, Nancy and Peter Rabinowitz, and Doug Raybeck. She will always be grateful for their commitment to excellent teaching and to helping young women be their best selves.

Judy Silverstein Gray, K'78
Judy Silverstein Gray credits her Kirkland education for inspiring several passions. While working in strategic communications, she authored six books and hundreds of articles focused on healthcare, history, and the environment. Serving three decades in the United States Coast Guard Reserves, she also developed expertise in community preparedness and pursued a Master's in Public Health. She is a kayaking enthusiast but spends her free time working on a creative nonfiction book about the advocacy of American POW wives during the Vietnam War.

Caroline BD Smith, '80
Caroline BD Smith, one-time features editor of the Hamilton/Kirkland *Spectator*, is a freelance writer specializing in biography and medical/scientific texts. She has a BA in English from Hamilton and an H.Dip. in Anglo-Irish Literature from Trinity College, Dublin. Based in London, she is currently working on a manuscript for a

book about her partner and his brother, singer-songwriter Yusuf Islam, formerly known as Cat Stevens. She has two children, Benjamin and Sarah.

Constance Stellas, K'72
Constance Stellas was a charter class member and since graduating has pursued a variety of careers. She is an actor and writer, with four published books and several short stories. For the past twenty years, Constance has been an astrologer. Her current project in development is a graphic novel series, *Tree of Keys*, which tells the tale of twelve orphans who become Astro Heroes based on the talents and challenges of their star signs.

Janet Sternberg, K'75
A native New Yorker raised in Rio de Janeiro, Brazil, Janet Sternberg earned her doctorate in media ecology with Neil Postman at New York University. She has taught at Cornell University, Fordham University, New York University, Queens College of the City University of New York, and Universidade de São Paulo. A former Fulbright scholar, she served as president of the Media Ecology Association and published *Misbehavior in Cyber Places*, a 2012 book about the regulation of conduct on the Internet. Her voice and words greet the Universe in Portuguese aboard the NASA Voyager Golden Record traveling through interstellar space.

Isabel Weinger Nielsen, K'76
Isabel Weinger Nielsen attended Kirkland College because of its creative writing program and did public relations for the Arts Division while there. Her senior project, *Portraits and Self-Portrait*, included "She Might Break," which won the Watrous Award for Fiction (1976)

and was published in *Lost Orchard* (2014). Isabel has worked as a book indexer, editor, freelance photographer, and administrative assistant at Norwich University. She wrote and edited an online newsletter for the College of Liberal Arts at Norwich and exhibits and sells photographs in Vermont. Isabel was married to, and inspired by, Lars Nielsen, '77, an honorary "Kirkie," who died in June 2018 and was a playwright and poet. She has two wonderful sons, Ari and Noah.

Julie Weinstein, K'75

Julie Weinstein, a born New Yorker, has a BA in Creative Writing, an MA in Counseling Psychology from Pepperdine University (1986), and an MS in Global Affairs from NYU (2012). In her first life, Julie worked as a community counseling center substance abuse counselor and as a supervisor for the Los Angeles Department of Children and Family Services with families involved with foster care. She returned to New York in 2009 and, missing the academic environment terribly, went back to school. Her focus within the Global Affairs program was alternative therapeutic interventions with refugees. In her second life, Julie teaches psychology at LaGuardia Community College (and taught English for Speakers of Other Languages). She has one daughter, who is an actor and playwright and lives in an amazing community-oriented apartment building (so reminiscent of Kirkland suites) with a view of the Hudson River and the George Washington Bridge.

Elaine F. Weiss, K'73

Elaine Weiss is a journalist and author, whose feature writing has been recognized with prizes from the Society of Professional Journalists and featured in many national publications. Her long-form writing won a Pushcart Prize "Editor's Choice" award, and she is a proud MacDowell Colony Fellow. After many years as a magazine writer and editor, she has turned to writing books of narrative history, especially in women's history. Her first book was *Fruits of Victory: The Woman's Land Army in the Great War* (University of Nebraska Press). Her most recent book, *The Woman's Hour: The Great Fight to Win the Vote* (Viking/Penguin) has won critical acclaim from *The New York Times, The Wall St. Journal,* and *The New Yorker. The Woman's Hour* was a GoodReads Readers' Choice Award winner, short-listed for the 2019 Chautauqua Prize, and received the American Bar Association's highest honor, the 2019 Silver Gavel Award. Steven Speilberg's Amblin production company is adapting the book for TV, with Hillary Rodham Clinton as Executive Producer. Elaine lives in Baltimore with her husband and two grown children. She relaxes by paddling her little kayak on Chesapeake Bay.

Elisabeth Weiss, K'80
Elisabeth Weiss teaches writing at Salem State University in Salem, MA. She's taught poetry in preschools, prisons, and nursing homes, as well as to the intellectually disabled. She's worked in the editorial department at Harper & Row in New York and has an MFA from The University of Iowa Writers Workshop. She's published poems in London's *Poetry Review, Porch, Crazyhorse, Birmingham Poetry Review, Paterson Literary Review,* and many other journals. Lis won the Talking Writing Hybrid Poetry Prize for 2016 and was a runner-up in the 2013 Boston Review poetry contest. Her chapbook, *The Caretaker's Lament*, was published by Finishing Line Press in 2016.

Acknowledgments

Thank you to everyone who helped me bring this book to fruition.

To my associate editors: Nancy Avery Dafoe, Elisabeth Horwitt, and Jo Pitkin.

For your support: Sharon Rippey, Maria Paula Zapata, Kathy Collett, Hamilton College Archives, Lucy Arnold, Jessica Temple, Pen Women Press, National League of American Pen Women, Inc., and Lars Nielsen.

To our many donors who contributed to funding, including: Debra A. Aidun, Elizabeth Aiman Swallow, Nancy Avery Dafoe, Phyllis J. Cohen, Diane C. Davis, Rebecca Eddy Feuerstein, Susan Greenblatt Neuffer, Elisabeth Horwitt-Putnam, Rebecca W. Johnson, Carol Kindig Urbanic, Dean Mitchell, Barbara Elizabeth Nixon, Sabrina I. Pacifi, Anne Rothwell Forlines, Lisa Sherman Wade, and the Susanne Marcus Collins Foundation.

To my creative writing teachers and mentors: Natalie Babbitt, Michael Burkhardt, David Rigsbee, Bill Rosenfeld, and Kathy Saltonstall Dewart.

The editors extend their grateful acknowledgment to the following sources for permission to reprint these selections:

Ashton Applewhite: "Having the Talk—not the one about sex, the one about dying" in *ThisChairRocks.com*, July 13, 2015.

Nancy Avery Dafoe: "My One Hundred Sisters" in *Toad Suck Review*, Issue #6, a literary journal published by the Department of Writing in the College of Fine Arts and Communication at the University of Central Arkansas, 2016.

Samuel Fisher Babbitt: Afterword in *Limited Engagement: Kirkland College 1965–1978: An Intimate History of the Rise and Fall of a Coordinate College for Women*, Xlibris, 2006.

Margaret Doris: "Mitt's Magic Underwear and the Granny Ass Dance" in *Esquire.com*, August 20, 2012.

Stephanie Feuer: "A Bench of One's Own," (earlier version) in *Write Place at the Write Time.org*.

Jane Gottlieb: "My House: Out of Fashion and Running Out of Time" in *Utne.com*, April 28, 2016.

Susan Hartman: "A New Life for Refugees, and the City They Adopted" in *The New York Times*, August 10, 2014.

Dorothy Irwin: "Years of High Hopes," adapted from *Years of High Hopes: A Portrait of British Guiana, 1952–1956, from an American Family's Letters Home*, Hansib Publications Limited, 2016. In the U.S., inscribed copies are available directly from the author at YearsOfHighHopes@gmail.com.

Abigail Johnson: "Women's Fight for Equal Rights Takes a Leap Forward" in *Nevada Appeal*, February 5, 2014.

Janet Sternberg: "Unstable Users: Displacement and Distraction as Perils of the Transition to Digital Media." Abstract for paper presented at Media in Transition 7 Conference "MiT7—Unstable Platforms: The Promise and Peril of Transition," Massachusetts Institute of Technology, Cambridge, MA, May 13-15, 2011.

A Note About the Title

The Kirkland College campus was built on an apple orchard, and the college's official seal featured a green apple tree with a leaf, a blossom, and an apple on a white background. The metaphor of the orchard, as reflected in the works of this volume, is perhaps not actually lost, but merely fallow.

A Note About the Typeface

Everything at Kirkland—from the bright Marimekko fabrics covering our furniture to the architecture of Ben Thompson—was meant to convey the college's innovative, fresh approach to education. Our publications, too, had a modern look that was consistent with the college's image. For the text of *Lost Orchard II*, we chose Calibri, a sans serif typeface similar to Optima which was chosen for *Lost Orchard I*. Calibri was designed by Luc(as) de Groot to make text clearer to read on liquid crystal display monitors. It was released to the public in 2007 with Microsoft Office and Windows Vista.

For More Information about Kirkland College

hamilton.edu/alumni/network/kirklandcollege/the-meaning-of-kirkland

Limited Engagement: Kirkland College 1965-1978: An Intimate History of the Rise & Fall of a Coordinate College for Women by Samuel Fisher Babbitt

Separate by Degree: Women's Students' Experiences in Single-Sex and Coeducational Colleges by Leslie Miller-Bernal

Going Coed: Women's Experiences in Formerly Men's Colleges and Universities, 1950-2000 by Leslie Miller-Bernal and Susan L. Poulson

9 781950 251018